£1.50

D1436524

JOHN SUCKLING

AGLAURA
1638

Scolar Press 1970

PRINTED AND PUBLISHED BY
SCOLAR PRESS LIMITED
20 MAIN STREET
MENSTON
ENGLAND

NOTE

Reproduced (original size) by permission of the Trustees of the British Museum. Shelf-mark: Ashley. 5058.

The first performance of *Aglaura* probably took place in the winter of 1638/39. It was an ostentatious production designed to attract attention as much by the amount of money which had been spent on it as by the play itself. Suckling was already notorious for his extravagant behaviour and the production of *Aglaura* increased his reputation and brought down stern criticism from the Puritans.

The appearance of the play in print caused further comment — it particularly upset Richard Brome (see "Upon Aglaura printed in Folio" in his *Five New Playes*, 1659). The normal procedure was to publish a single play in a reasonably cheap quarto edition and to reserve the folio format for collected editions. Suckling, however, first published *Aglaura* as a folio (reproduced here).

Interest in *Aglaura* continued for many years after its first appearance and also after Suckling's death (in 1642 either by suicide or murder). It was reprinted in *Fragmenta Aurea* 1646, 1648, and 1658-59, and in *The Works of Sir John Suckling*, 1676, and 1696 (where the title-pages to *Aglaura* are dated 1694), and from contemporary records it is known that performances were still taking place in 1691.

There is a manuscript version in the British Museum (MS.Royal.18.C.xxv) in which the play ends as a tragedy. This manuscript was probably a presentation copy for the first performance and Suckling must have been persuaded afterwards to give his play a happy ending since the printed versions are provided with the original tragic ending and an alternative last act which ends happily.

There have been modern editions by W. C. Hazlitt in *The Poems, Plays and Other Remains*, 1874, and A. H. Thompson in *Works*, 1910. See also G. E. Bentley *The Jacobean and Caroline Stage*, 5 Vols., 1956.

Reference: STC 23420.

AGLAURA.

LONDON,
Printed by *Iohn Haviland* for *Thomas Walkley*, and are
to be sold at his shop at the Signe of the Flying
Horse betweene York-house
and Britaines Burse. 1638.

Aprilis 18. 1638.
Imprimatur, MATTH. CLAY.

PROLOGVE.

I'Ve thought upon't ; and cannot tell which way
Ought I can say now, should advance the Play.
For Playes are either good, or bad ; the good,
(If they doe beg) beg to be underſtood.
And in good faith, that has as bold a ſound,
As if a beggar ſhould aske twentie pound.
———— Men have it not about them :
Then (Gentlemen) if rightly underſtood,
The bad doe need leſſe Prologue than the good :
For if it chance the Plot be lame, or blinde,
Ill cloath'd, deform'd throughout, it needs muſt finde
Compaſſion, ———— It is a beggar without Art :————
But it fals out in penny worths of Wit,
As in all bargaines elſe. Men ever get
All they can in ; will have London meaſure,
A handfull over in their verie pleaſure.
And now yee have't ; hee could not well deny'ee,
And I dare ſweare hee's ſcarce a ſaver by yee.

Prologue to the Court.

THoſe common paſſions, hopes, and feares, that ſtill,
The Poets firſt and then the Prologues fill
In this our age, hee that writ this, by mee,
Proteſts againſt as modeſt foolerie.
Hee thinks it an odd thing to be in paine,
For nothing elſe, but to be well againe.
Who writes to feare is ſo ; had hee not writ,
You nere had been the Iudges of his wit ;
And when hee had, did hee but then intend
To pleaſe himſelfe, hee ſure might have his end
Without th'expence of hope, and that hee had
That made this Play, although the Play be bad.
Then Gentlemen be thriftie, ſave your doomes
For the next man, or the next Play that comes ;
For ſmiles are nothing, where men doe not care,
And frownes as little, where they need not feare.

To the King.

THis (Sir) to them, but unto Majeſtie.
All hee has ſaid before, hee does denie.
Yet not to Majeſtie : that were to bring
His feares to be, but for the Queene and King,
Not for your ſelves ; and that hee dares not ſay :
Y'are his Soveraignes another way :
Your ſoules are Princes, and you have as good
A title that way, as yee have by blood
To governe, and here your powers more great
And abſolute, than in the royall Seat.
There men diſpute, and but by Law obey,
Here is no Law at all, but what yee ſay.

Scena

Scena Perfia.

KING, *In love with* Aglaura.

THERSAMES, *Prince, in love with* Aglaura.

ORBELLA, *Queene, at firſt Miſtreſſe to* Ziriff : *in love with* Ariaſpes.

ARIASPES, *Brother to the King.*

ZIRIFF, *Otherwayes* Sorannez *diſguiſed, Captaine of the Guard, in love with* Orbella, *brother to* Aglaura.

JOLAS, *A Lord of the Councell, ſeeming friend to the Prince, but a Traytour, in love with* Semanthe.

AGLAURA, *In love with the Prince, but nam'd Miſtreſſe to the King.*

ORSAMES, *A young Lord antiplatonique ; friend to the Prince.*

PHILAN, *The ſame.*

SEMANTHE, *In love with* Ziriff; *platonique.*

ORITHIE, *In love with* Therſames.

PASITHAS, *A faithfull ſervant.*

JOLINAS, Aglaura's *waiting-woman.*

COURTIERS.

HUNTSMEN.

PRIEST.

GUARD.

AGLAURA.

ACTUS I. SCENA I.

Enter JOLAS, JOLINA.

JOLAS, Married? and in *Diana's* Grove!
  JOLIN. So was th'appointment, or my Senfe deceiv'd me.
  JOLAS, Married!
  Now by thofe Powers that tye thofe prettie knots,
  'tis verie fine, good faith 'tis wondrous fine:
JOLIN. What is, Brother?
JOLAS, Why? to marrie Sifter———
t'injoy 'twixt lawfull and unlawfull thus
a happineffe, fteale as 'twere ones owne;
Diana's Grove, fayeft thou?——— *Scratcheth his head.*
  JOLIN. That's the place; the hunt once up, and all
ingag'd in the fport, they meane to leave
the company, and fteale unto thofe thickets,
where, there's a Prieft attends them;
  JOLAS, And will they lye together, think'ft thou?
  JOLIN. Is there diftinction of fex thinke you?
or flefh and bloud?
  JOLAS, True; but the King, Sifter!
  JOLIN. But love, Brother!
  JOLAS, Thou fayeft well;
'tis fine, 'tis wondrous fine:
    Diana's grove———
  JOLIN. Yes, *Diana's* grove,
but brother if you fhould fpeake of this now,
  JOLAS, Why thou know'ft a drowning man holds not a thing fo faft:
Semanthe! fhe fhuns me too: *Enter* Semanthe, *fhe fees*
  JOLIN. The wound feftred fure!   Jolas, *and goes in agen.*
the hurt the boy gave her, when firft
fhee look'd abroad into the world, is not yet cur'd.
  JOLAS, What hurt?
  JOLIN. Why, know you not
fhee was in love long fince with young *Zorannes*,
(*Aglaura's* brother,) and the now Queenes betroth'd?
  JOLAS, Some fuch flight Tale I've heard.
  JOLIN. Slight? fhe yet does weepe, when fhe but heares him nam'd;
and tels the prettieft and the faddeft ftories
of all thofe civill wars, and thofe Amours,
That, truft me, both my Lady and my felfe
turne weping Statues ftill.
  JOLAS, Pifh, 'tis not that.
'Tis *Ziriff*, and his frefh glories here
have robb'd me of her.
Since he thus appear'd in Court,
my love has languifh'd worfe than Plants in drought.
But time's a good Phyfician: come, lets in:
the King and Queene by this time are come forth.   *Exeunt.*

Enter Serving-men to Ziriff.

1 SERV. Yonder's a crowd without, as if some strange sight
were to be seene to day here.

2 SERV. Two or three with Carbonadoes afore in stead of faces
mistooke the doore for a breach, and at the opening of it,
are striving still which should enter first.

3 SERV. Is my Lord busie ?   (*Knocks.*)

Enter Ziriff *as in his Studie.*

1 SERV. My Lord, there are some Souldiers without———

ZIR. Well, I will dispatch them presently.

2 SERV. Th'Embassadours from the Cadusians too———

ZIR. Shew them the Gallerie.

3 SERV. One from the King———

ZIR. Againe ? I come, I come.   *Exeunt Serving-men.*

Ziriff *solus.*

Greatnesse, thou vainer shadow of the Princes beames,
begot by meere reflection, nourish'd in extreames ;
first taught to creepe, and live upon the glance,
poorely to fare, till thine owne proper strength
bring thee to surfet of thy selfe at last.
How dull a Pageant, would this States-play seeme
to mee now ; were not my love and my revenge
mixt with it ?———
Three tedious Winters have I waited here,
like patient Chymists blowing still the coales,
and still expecting, when the blessed houre
would come, should make me master of
the Court *Elixar,* Power, for that turnes all :
'tis in projection now ; downe, sorrow, downe,
and swell my heart no more, and thou wrong'd ghost
of my dead father, to thy bed agen,
and sleepe securely ;
it cannot now be long, for sure *Fate* must,
as't has beene cruell, so, a while be just.   *Exit.*

Enter King and Lords, the Lords intreating for Prisoners.

KING. I say they shall not live ; our mercie !
would turne sinne, should we but use it er'e :
Pittie, and Love, the bosses onely be
of government, merely for shew and ornament.
Feare is the bit that mans proud will restraines,
and makes its vice its vertue———See it done.

Enter to them Queene, Aglaura, *Ladies, the King addresses*
himselfe to Aglaura.

So early, and so curious in your dresse, (faire Mistresse ?)
these prettie ambushes and traps for hearts
set with such care to day, looke like designe :
speake, Lady, is't a massacre resolv'd ?
is conquering one by one growne tedious sport ?
or is the number of the taken such,
that for your safetie you must kill out-right ?

AGL. Did none doe greater mischiefe (Sir) than I,
heav'n would not much be troubled with sad storie,
nor would the quarrell man has to the Starres
be kept alive so strongly.

KING. When hee does leave't
woman must take it up, and justly too ;

for

for robbing of the fex and giving all to you.

AGL. Their weakneffes you meane, and I confeffe, Sir.

KING. The greateft fubjects of their power or glorie.
Such gentle rape thou act'ft upon my foule,
and with fuch pleafing violence doft force it ftill;
that when it fhould refift, it tamely yeilds,
making a kinde of hafte to be undone,
as if the way to victorie were loffe,
and conqueft came by overthrow.

Enter an Expreffe delivering a Packet upon his knee.
The King reads.

QU. Prettie!   *The Queene looking upon a flower in one of the Ladies heads.*
Is it the child of nature, or of fome faire hand?

LA. 'Tis as the beautie Madam of fome faces,
Arts iffue onely.

KING. *Therfames,*
This concernes you moft, brought you her picture?

EXP. Something made up for her in hafte I have.   *Prefents the Picture.*

KING. If fhe does owe no part of this faire dower
unto the Painter, fhe is rich enough.

AGL. A kinde of merrie fadneffe in this face
becomes it much.

KING. There is indeed, *Aglavra,*
a prettie fullenneffe dreft up in fmiles,
that fayes this beautie can both kill, and fave.
How like you her *Therfames?*

THER. As well as any man can doe a houfe
by feeing of the portall, here's but a face,
and faces (Sir) are things I have not ftudied;
I have my dutie, and may boldly fweare,
what you like beft will ever pleafe me moft.

KING. Spoke like *Therfames,* and my fonne,
come! the day holds faire,
let all the Huntf-men meet us in the vale,
we will uncouple there.   *Exeunt.*

Ariafpes : folus ftayes behinde.

ARIASP. How odd a thing a croud is unto me!
fure nature intended I fhould be alone,
had not that old doting man-mid-wife *Time*
flept, when he fhould have brought me forth, I had
beene fo too ——— *Studies and fcratches his head.*
To be borne neere, and onely neere a crowne ——

Enter Jolas.

JOL. How now my Lord?
what? walking o'th' tops of Pyramids?
whifpering your felfe away
like a deny'd lover? come! to horfe, to horfe,
and I will fhew you ftreight a fight fhall pleafe you
more than kinde lookes from her you dote upon
after a falling out.

ARIASP. Prithee what is't?

JOL. Ile tell you as I goe.——— *Exeunt.*

Enter Huntf-men hollowing and whooping.

HUNT. Which way? which way?

Enter Therfames, Aglaura muffled.

THER. This is the grove, 'tis fomewhere here within.——   *Exeunt.*

Enter

Enter dogging of them, Ariaspes, Jolas.

JOL. Gently! Gently!

Enter Orsames, Philan, *a Huntsman, two Courtiers.*

HUNTS. No hurt, my Lord, I hope.

ORS. None, none,
Thou wouldst have warranted it to another,
if I had broke my neck :
what ? do'st thinke my horse and I shew tricks ?
that which way soever he throwes me
like a Tumblers boy I must fall safe ?
was there a bed of roses there ? would I were Eunuch if I had not as lief h'a falne
in the state, as where I did ; the ground was as hard, as if it had been pav'd with Pla-
tonicke Ladies hearts, and this unconscionable fellow askes whether I have no hurt;
where's my horse ?

1 COURT. Making love to the next mare I thinke.

2 COURT. Not the next I assure you,
hee's gallop't away, as if all the spurs i'th' field
were in his sides.

ORS. Why there's it : the jade's in the fashion too.
Now h'as done me an injurie, he will not come neere me.
Well when I hunt next, may it be upon a starv'd cow,
without a saddle too.
And may I fall into a saw-pit, and not be taken up, but with suspition of having
beene private, with mine owne beast there. Now I better consider on't too, Gentlemen, 'tis but the same thing we doe at Court; here's everie man striving who shall
be formost, and hotly pursuing of what he seldome overtakes, or if he does, it's no
great matter.

PHI. He that's best hors'd (that is best friended) gets in soonest, and then all hee
has to doe is to laugh at those that are behind. Shall we help you my Lord ?——

ORS. Prithee doe——stay !
To be in view, is to be in favour,
is it not ?

PHI. Right,
and he that has a strong faction against him, hunts upon a cold sent, and may in time
come to a losse.

ORS. Here's one rides two miles about, while another leapes a ditch and is in before him.

PHI. Where note the indirect way's the nearest.

ORS. Good againe——

PHI. And here's another puts on, and fals into a quagmire, (that is) followes
the Court till he has spent all (for your Court quagmire is want of money) there a
man is sure to stick, and then not one helps him out, if they doe not laugh at him.

1 COURT. What thinke you of him, that hunts after my rate
and never sees the Deere ?

2 COURT. Why hee is like some young fellow, that followes the Court, and
never sees the King.

ORS. To spurre a horse till he is tir'd, is

PHI. To importune a friend till he be wearie of you.

ORS. For then upon the first occasion y'are throwne off, as I was now.

PHI. This is nothing to the catching of your horse *Orsames.*

ORS. Thou say'st true, I thinke he is no transmigrated Philosopher, and therefore not likely to be taken with moralls.
Gentlemen——your help, the next I hope will bee yours, and then 'twill bee my
turne.——   *Exeunt.*

Enter againe married, Thersames, Aglaura; *Priest.*

THERS. Feare not my Deare, if when Loves diet

was bare lookes and thofe ftolne too,
he yet did thrive ! what then
will he doe now ? when everie night will be
a feaft, and everie day frefh revelrie.

AGL. Will he not furfet, when he once fhall come
to groffer fare (my Lord) and fo grow ficke,
and Love once ficke, how quickly will it dye ?

THER. Ours cannot; 'tis as immortall as the things
that elemented it, which were our foules :
nor can they ere impaire in health, for what
thefe holy rites doe warrant us to doe,
more than our bodies would for quenching thirft.
Come let's to horfe, we fhall be mift:
for we are envies marke, and Court eyes carrie farre.
Your prayers and filence Sir: —— *to the Prieft.*   ***Exeunt.***

Enter Ariafpes, Jolas.

ARI. If it fucceed ? I weare thee here my *Iolas* ———

JOL. If it fucceed ? will night fucceed the day ?
or houres one to another ? is not his luft
the Idoll of his foule ? and was not fhe
the Idoll of his luft ? as fafely he might
have ftolne the Diadem from off his head,
and he would leffe have mift it.
You now, my Lord, muft raife his jealoufie,
teach it to looke through the falfe opticke feare,
and make it fee all double : Tell him the Prince
would not have thus prefum'd, but that he does
intend worfe yet; and that his crowne and life
will be the next attempt.

ARI. Right, and I will urge
how dangerous 'tis unto the prefent ftate,
To have the creatures, and the followers
of the next Prince (whom all now ftrive to pleafe)
too neere about him :

JOL. What if the male-contents that ufe
to come unto him were difcovered ?

ARI. By no meanes; for 'twere in vaine to give
him difcontent (which too muft needs be done)
if they within him gave't not nourifhment.

JOL. Well, Ile away firft, for the print's too big
if we be feene together.————   ***Exit.***

ARI. I have fo fraught this Barke with hope, that it
dares venture now in any ftorme, or weather;
and if hee finke or fplits, all's one to me.
" Ambition feemes all things, and yet is none,
" but in difguife ftalkes to opinion
" and fooles it into faith, for everie thing :
'Tis not with th'afcending to a Throne,
As 'tis with ftaires, and fteps, that are the fame;
For to a Crowne, each humor's a degree;
and as men change, and differ, fo muft wee.
The name of vertue doth the people pleafe,
not for their love to vertue, but their eafe,
and Parrat Rumour I that tale have taught:
By making love I hold the womans grace,
'tis the Court double key, and entrance gets

C

to all the little plots; the fierie spirits
my love to Armes hath drawne into my faction;
all, but the minion of the Time, is mine,
and he shall be, or shall not be at all.
He that beholds a wing in pieces torne,
and knowes not that to heav'n it once did beare
the high-flowne and selfe-less'ning bird, will think
and call them idle Subjects of the winde:
when he that has the skill to imp and binde
these in right places, will thus truth discover;
That borrowed Instruments doe oft convey
the Soule to her propos'd Intents, and where
our Stars deny, Art may supply ——   *Exit.*
                Enter Semanthe, Orithie, Orsames, Philan.

SEM. Thinke you it is not then
the little jealousies (my Lord) and feares,
joy mixt with doubt, and doubt reviv'd with hope
that crownes all love with pleasure? these are lost
when once wee come to full fruition;
like waking in the morning when all night
our fancie has beene fed with some new strange delight.

ORS. I grant you, Madam, that the feares, and joyes,
hopes, and desires, mixt with despaires, and doubts,
doe make the sport in love; that they are
the verie dogs by which we hunt the hare;
but as the dogs would stop, and streight give o're
were it not for the little thing before;
so would our passions; both alike must be
flesh't in the chase.

ORI. Will you then place the happinesse, but there,
where the dull plow-man and the plow-mans horse
can finde it out? Shall soules refin'd, not know
how to preserve alive a noble flame,
but let it die, burne out to appetite?

SEM. Love's a Chamelion, and would live on aire,
Physick for agues, starving is his food.

ORS. Why? there's it now! a greater Epicure
lives not on earth; my Lord and I have beene
in's privie kitchin, seene his bills of Fare.

SEM. And how, and how my Lord?

ORS. A mightie Prince,
and full of curiositie —— Harts newly slaine
serv'd up intire, and stucke with little Arrowes
in stead of Cloves ——

PHI. Sometimes a cheeke plumpt up
with broth, with creame and clarret mingled
for sauce, and round about the dish
Pomegranate kernells, strew'd on leaves of Lillies.

ORS. Then will he have black eies, for those of late
he feeds on much, and for varietie
the gray ——

PHI. You forget his cover'd dishes
of Iene-straves, and Marmalade of lips,
perfum'd by breath sweet as the beanes first blossomes.

SEM. Rare!
And what's the drinke to all this meat, my Lord?

ORS. Nothing but pearle diſſolv'd, teares ſtill freſh fetch'd
from Lovers eyes, which if they come to be
warme in the carriage, are ſtreight cool'd with ſighs.

SEM. And all this rich proportion, perchance
we would allow him :

ORS. True ! but therefore this is but his common diet ;
onely ſerves
when his chiefe Cookes, *Liking* and *Opportunitie,*
are out o'th' way ; for when hee feaſts indeed,
'tis there, where the wiſe people of the world
did place the vertues, i'th' middle —— Madam.

ORI. My Lord, there is ſo little hope we ſhould convert you,
and if we ſhould, ſo little got by it,
that wee'll not loſe ſo much upon't as ſleepe.
Your Lordſhips ſervants ———

ORS. Nay Ladies wee'll wait upon you to your chambers.

PH. Prithee lets ſpare the complement, we ſhall doe no good.

ORS. By this hand Ile try,
they keepe me faſting, and I muſt be praying.   *Exeunt.*

Aglaura undreſſing of her ſelfe, Jolina.

AGL. Undreſſe mee : ——
Is it not late, *Iolina?*
it was the longeſt day, this ———

Enter Therſames.

THER. Softly, as Death it ſelfe comes on,
when it does ſteale away the ſicke mans breath,
and ſtanders by perceive it not,
have I trod the way unto theſe lodgings.
How wiſely doe thoſe Powers
that give us happineſſe, order it ?
ſending us ſtill feares to bound our joyes,
which elſe would over-flow and loſe themſelves :
ſee where ſhee ſits,
like Day retir'd into another world.
Deare mine ! where all the beautie man admires
in ſcattered pieces, does united lye.
Where ſenſe does feaſt, and yet where ſweet deſire
lives in its longing, like a miſers eye,
that never knew, nor ſaw ſacietie :
tell me, by what approaches muſt I come
to take in what remaines of my felicitie?

AGL. Needs there any new ones, where the breach
is made already ? you are entred here ——
long ſince (Sir) here, and I have giv'n up all.

THER. All but the Fort, and in ſuch wars, as theſe,
till that be yeilded up, there is no peace,
nor triumph to be made ; come ! undoe, undoe,
and from theſe envious clouds ſlide quicke
into Loves proper Sphere, thy bed :
The wearie traveller, whom the buſie Sunne
hath vex't all day, and ſcortch'd almoſt to tinder,
nere long'd for night, as I have long'd for this.
What rude hand is that ?   *One knocks haſtily.*
Goe *Iolina,* ſee, but let none enter ——   *Iolina goes to the doore.*

JOL. 'Tis *Ziriff,* Sir.

THER. —— Oh ——

Something of weight hath falne out it seemes,
which in his zeale he could not keepe till morning.
But one short minute, Deare, into that chamber. ——

Enter Ziriff.

How now?
thou start'st, as if thy sinnes had met thee,
or thy Fathers ghost; what newes man?

ZIR. Such as will send the blood of hastie messages
unto the heart, and make it call
all that is man about you into councell;
where's the Princesse, Sir?

THER. Why? what of her?

ZIR. The King must have her——

THER. How?

ZIR. The King must have her (Sir)

THER. Though feare of worse makes ill, still relish better,
and this looke handsome in our friendship, *Ziriff,*
yet so severe a preparation——
there needed not: come, come! what ist?

Ziriff leads him to the doore, and shewes him a Guard.

A Guard! *Thersames,*
thou art lost; betray'd
by faithlesse and ungratefull man,
out of a happinesse:——   *He steps betweene the doore and him, and drawes.*
the verie thought of that,
will lend my anger so much noble justice,
that wert thou master of as much fresh life,
as th'ast beene of villany, it should not serve,
nor stocke thee out, to glorie, or repent
the least of it.

ZIR. Put up: put up! such unbecomming anger
I have not seene you weare before.
What? draw upon your friend,   *Discovers himselfe.*
doe you beleeve me right now? ——

THER. I scarce beleeve mine eyes: —— *Zorannes.*

ZIR. The same, but how preserv'd, or why
thus long disguis'd to you, a freer houre must speake:
That y'are betrai'd is certaine, but by whom,
unlesse the Priest himselfe, I cannot ghesse
more than the marriage, though he knowes not of:
if you now send her on these early summons
before the sparks are growne into a flame,
you doe redeeme th'offence, or make it lesse;
and (on my life) yet his intents are faire,
and he will but besiege, not force affection.
So you gaine time; if you refuse, there's but
one way; you know his power and passion.

THER. Into how strange a labyrinth am I
now falne! what shall I doe *Zorannes?*

ZIR. Doe (Sir) as Sea-men, that have lost their light
and way: strike saile, and lye quiet a while.
Your forces in the Province are not yet
in readinesse, nor is our friend *Zephines*
arriv'd at Delphos; nothing is ripe, besides——

THER. Good heavens, did I but dreame that she was mine?
upon imagination did I climbe up to

this

this height ? let mee then wake and dye,
fome courteous hand fnatch mee from what's to come,
and ere my wrongs have being, give them end :

ZIR. How poore, and how unlike the Prince is this ?
this trifle woman does unman us all ;
robs us fo much, it makes us things of pittie.
Is this a time to loofe our anger in ?
and vainly breathe it out ? when all wee have
will hardly fill the faile of Refolution,
and make us beare up high enough for action.

THER. I have done (Sir) pray chide no more ;
the flave whom tedious cuftome has enur'd
and taught to thinke of miferie as of food,
counting it but a neceffarie of life,
and fo digefting it, fhall not fo much as once
be nam'd to patience, when I am fpoken of :
marke mee ; for I will now undoe my felfe
as willingly, as virgins give up all firft nights
to them they love :——— *Offers to goe out.*

ZIR. Stay, Sir, 'twere fit *Aglaura* yet were kept
in ignorance : I will difmiffe the Guard,
and be my felfe againe. *Exit.*

THER. In how much worfe eftate am I in now,
Than if I nere had knowne her ; privation,
is a miferie as much above bare wretchedneffe,
as that is fhort of happineffe :
So when the Sunne does not appeare,
'Tis darker 'caufe it once was here.

Enter Ziriff *fpeakes to* Orfames *and others halfe entred.*

ZIR. Nay, Gentlemen :
there needs no force, where there is no refiftance :
Ile fatisfie the King my felfe.

THER. ———Oh 'tis well y'are come,
there was within me frefh Rebellion,
and reafon was almoft unking'd agen,
But you fhall have her Sir —— *Goes out to fetch* Aglaura.

ZIR. What doubtfull combats in this noble youth
paffion and reafon have ! ———

Enter Therfames *leading* Aglaura.

THER. Here Sir—— *Gives her, goes out.*

AGL. What meanes the Prince, my Lord ?

ZIR. Madam, his wifer feare has taught him to difguife
his love, and make it looke a little rude at parting.
Affaires that doe concenre, all that you hope from
happineffe, this night force him away :
and left you fhould have tempted him to ftay,
(Which hee did doubt you would and would prevaile)
he left you thus : he does defire by mee
you would this night lodge in the little towre,
which is in my command ; the reafons why
himfelfe will fhortly tell you.

AGL. 'Tis ftrange, but I am all Obedience —— *Exeunt.*

ACTUS II. SCENA I.

Enter Therfames, Jolas a Lord of the Counfell.

JOL. I told him fo, Sir, urg'd 'twas no common knot,
that to the tying of it two powerfull Princes,
Vertue and Love were joyn'd, and that
a greater than thefe two was now
ingaged in it ; Religion, but 'twould not doe,
the corke of paffion.boy'd up all reafon fo
that what was faid, fwam but o'th' top of th'eare
nere reach't the heart :

THER. Is there no way for Kings to fhew their power,
but in their Subjects wrongs ? no fubject neither
but his owne fonne ?

JOL. Right Sir :
no quarrie for his luft to gorge on, but on what
you fairely had flowne at, and taken :
well——wert not the King, or wert indeed
not you, that have fuch hopes, and fuch a crowne
to venter, and yet———
'tis but a woman.

THER. How ? that but againe, and thou art more injurious
than hee, and woul't provoke me fooner.

JOL. Why Sir ?
there are no altars yet addreft unto her,
nor facrifice ; if I have made her leffe
thanwhat fhe is, it'was my love to you :
For in my thoughts, and here within, I hold her
the nobleft peece Nature ere lent our eyes,
and of the which, all women elfe, are but
weake counterfeits, made up by her journey-men :
but was this fit to tell you ?
I know you value but too high all that,
and in a loffe we fhould not make things more,
'tis miferies happineffe, that wee can make it leffe
by art, throw a forgetfulneffe upon our ills,
Yet who can doe it here ?
when everie voyce, muft needs, and everie face,
by fhewing what fhe was not, fhew what fhe was.

THER. Ile inftantly unto him.——*drawes.*

JOL. Stay Sir :
Though't be the utmoft of my Fortunes hope
to have an equall fhare of ill with you :
yet I could wifh we fold this trifle life,
at a farre dearer rate, than we are like to doe,
fince 'tis a King's the Merchant.

THER. Ha !
King, I ! 'tis indeed,
and there's no Art can cancell that high bond :

JOL. ——Hee cooles againe.—— *(to himfelfe.)*
True Sir, and yet mee thinks to know a reafon——
for paffive nature nere had glorious end,
and he that States preventions ever learn'd,
knowes, 'tis one motion to ftrike and to defend.

Enter

Enter Serving-man.

SERV. Some of the Lords without, and from the King,
they say, wait you.

THER. What subtle State tricke now ?
but one turne here, and I am back my Lord.——*Exit.*

JOL. This will not doe; his refolution's like
a skilfull horfe-man, and reafon is the ftirrop,
which though a fudden fhock may make
it loofe, yet does it meet it handfomely agen.
Stay, 'tmuft be fome fudden feare of wrong
to her, that may draw on a fudden act
from him, and ruine from the King; for fuch
a fpirit will not like common ones, be
rais'd by everie fpell, 'tis in loves circle
onely 'twill appeare.

Enter Therfames.

THER. I cannot beare the burthen of my wrongs
one minute longer.

JOL. Why *!* what's the matter Sir ?

THER. They doe pretend the fafetie of the State
now, nothing but my marriage with *Cadufia*
can fecure th'adjoyning countrey to it;
confinement during life for me if I refufe
Diana's Nunnerie for her —— And at that Nunn'rie, *Iolus*,
allegiance in mee like the ftring of a watch
wound up too high, and forc'd above the nicke,
ran backe, and in a moment was unravell'd all.

JOL. Now by the love I beare to Juftice,
That Nunn'rie was too fevere; when vertuous love's a crime
what man can hope to fcape a punifhment,
or who's indeed fo wretched to defire it ?

THER. Right !

JOL. What anfwer made you, Sir ?

THER. None, they gave me till to morrow,
and ere that be, or they or I
muft know our deftinie :
come friend let's in, there is no fleeping now;
for time is fhort, and we have much to doe.——*Exeunt.*

Enter Orfames, Philan, *Courtiers.*

ORS. Judge you, Gentlemen, if I be not as unfortunate
as a gamefter thinks himfelfe upon the loffe
of the laft ftake; this is the firft fhe
I ever fwore to heartily, and (by thofe eyes)
I thinke I had continued unperjur'd a whole moneth,
(and that's faire you'll fay.)

1 COURT. Verie faire———

ORS. Had fhe not run mad betwixt.———

2 COURT. How ? mad ?
who ? *Semanthe* ?

ORS. Yea, yea, mad, aske *Philan* elfe.
people that want cleere intervalls talke not
fo wildly: Ile tell you Gallants; 'tis now, fince firft I found my felfe a little hot,
and quivering 'bout the heart, fome ten dayes fince, (a tedious Ague) Sirs; (but
what of that ?)
the gratious glance, and little whifper paft,
approches made from th'hand unto the lip,

i came

I came to vifit her, and (as you know we ufe)
breathing a figh or two by way of prologue,
told her, that in Loves Phyficke 'twas a rule,
where the difeafe had birth to feeke a cure ;
I had no fooner nam'd love to her, but fhe
began to talke of Flames, and Flames,
neither devouring, nor devour'd, of Aire,
and of Camelions ———

    1 Court. Oh the *Platoniques.*

    2 Court. Thofe of the new religion in love ! your Lordfhip's merrie,
troth, how doe you like the humor on't ?

    Ors. As thou would'ft like red haire, or leanneffe
in thy Miftreffe; fcurvily, 'tdoes worfe with handfomneffe,
than ftrong defire would doe with impotence;
a meere tricke to inhance the price of kiffes ———

    Phi. Sure thefe filly women, when they feed
our expectation fo high, doe but like
ignorant Conjurers, that raife a Spirit
which handfomly they cannot lay againe :

    Ors. True, 'tis like fome that nourifh up
young Lions till they grow fo great, they are affraid of themfelves, they dare not
grant at laft,
for feare they fhould not fatisfie.

    Phi. Who's for the Towne ? I muft take up againe,

    Ors. This villanous Love's as chargeable as the Philofophers Stone, and thy
Miftreffe as hard to compaffe too !

    Phi. The Platonique is ever fo ; they are as tedious
before they come to the point, as an old man
fall'n into the Stories of his youth;

    2. Cour. Or a widow into the praifes of her firft husband.

    Ors. Well, if fhe hold out but one moneth longer,
if I doe not quite forget, I ere beleaguer'd there,
and remove the fiege to another place, may all
the curfes beguil'd virgins lofe upon their perjur'd Lovers
fall upon mee.

    Phi. And thou woult deferve 'em all.

    Ors. For what ?

    Phi. For being in the company of thofe
that tooke away the Prince's Miftreffe from him.

    Ors. Peace, that will be redeem'd ———
I put but on this wildneffe to difgu'fe my felfe ;
there are brave things in hand, hearke i'thy eare : ——*(Whifper)*

    1. Court. Some fevere plot upon a maiden-head.
Thefe two young Lords make love,
as Embroyderers worke againft a Maske, night and day ;
They thinke importunitie a neerer way than merit,
and take women as Schoole-boyes catch Squirrells.
hunt 'em up and downe till they are wearie,
and fall downe before 'em.

    Ors. Who loves the Prince failes not ———

    Phi. And I am one : my injuries are great as thine,
and doe perfwade as ftrongly.

    Ors. I had command to bring thee,
faile not and in thine owne difguife

    Phi. Why in difguife ?

    Ors. It is the Princes policie and love ;

for if wee fhould mifcarrie,
fome one taken might betray the reft
unknowne to one another,
each man is fafe, in his owne valour;

2. COURT. And what Mercers wife are you to cheapen now
in ftead of his filks?

ORS. Troth; 'tis not fo well; 'tis but a Cozen of thine——
come *Philan* let's along:—— *Exeunt.*

Enter Queene alone.

ORB. What is it thus within whifpering remorfe,
and calls Love Tyrant? all powers, but his,
their rigour, and our feare, have made divine!
But everie Creature holds of him by fenfe,
the fweeteft Tenure; yea! but my husbands brother:
and what of that? doe harmleffe birds or beafts
aske leave of curious Heraldrie at all?
Does not the wombe of one faire fpring,
bring unto the earth many fweet rivers,
that wantonly doe one another chace,
and in one bed, kiffe, mingle, and embrace?
Man (Natures heire) is not by her will ti'de,
to fhun all creatures are alli'd unto him,
for then hee fhould fhun all; fince death and life
doubly allies all them that live by breath:
The Aire that does impart to all lifes brood,
refrefhing, is fo neere to it felfe, and to us all,
that all in all is individuall:
But, how am I fure one and the fame defire
warmes *Ariafpes*: for Art can keepe alive
a beddred love.

Enter Ariafpes.

ARI. Alone, (Madam) and overcaft with thought,
uncloud--uncloud--for if wee may beleeve
the fmiles of Fortune, love fhall no longer pine
in prifon thus, nor undelivered travell
with throes of feare, and of defire about it.
The Prince, (like to a valiant beaft in nets)
ftriving to force a freedome fuddenly,
has made himfelfe at length, the furer prey:
the King ftands only now betwixt, and is,
juft like a fingle tree, that hinders all the profpect:
'tis but the cutting downe of him, and wee ——

ORB. Why would't thou thus imbarque into ftrange feas,
and trouble Fate, for what wee have already?
Thou art to mee what thou now feek'ft, a Kingdome;
and were thy love as great, as thy ambition;
I fhould be fo to thee.

ARI. Thinke you, you are not Madam?
as well and juftly may you doubt the truths,
tortur'd, or dying men doe leave behinde them:
but then my fortune turnes my miferie,
when my addition fhall but make you leffe;
fhall I endure that head that wore a crowne,
for my fake fhould weare none? Firft let mee lofe
th'exchequer of my wealth, your love; nay, may
all that rich Treafurie you have about you,

E

be rifled by the man I hated, and I looke on;
though youth be full of sinne, and heav'n be juft,
so sad a doome I hope they keepe not from me;
Remember what a quicke Apoftacie he made,
when all his vowes were up to heav'n and you.
How, ere the Bridall torches were burnt out,
his flames grew weake, and ficklier; thinke on that,
thinke how unfafe you are, if she should now,
not fell her honour at a lower rate,
than your place in his bed.

    ORB. And would not you prove falfe too then?
    ARI. By this-- and this-- loves break-faft: (*Kiffes her.*)
by his feafts too yet to come, by all the
beautie in this face, divinitie too great
tobe prophan'd ———

    ORB. O doe not fweare by that;
Cankers may eat that flow'r upon the ftalke,
(for ficknefle and mifchance, are great devourers)
and when there is not in thefe cheeks and lips,
left red enough to blufh at perjurie,
when you fhall make it, what fhall I doe then?

    ARI. Our foules by that time (Madam)
will by long cuftome fo acquainted be,
they will not need that duller truch-man Flefh,
but freely, and without thofe poorer helps,
converfe and mingle; meane time wee'll teach
our loves to fpeake, not thus to live by fignes,
and action is his native language, Madam,
             Enter Ziriff *unfeene.*
this box but open'd to the Senfe will doe't.

    ORB. I undertake I know not what,
    ARI. Thine owne fafetie (Deareft)
let it be this night, if thou do'ft;   *Whisper and kiffe.*
love thy felfe or mee.

    ORB. That's verie fudden.
    ARI. Not if wee be fo, and we muft now be wife,
For when their Sunne fets, ours begins to rife.—— *Exeunt.*
              Ziriff *folus.*

    ZIR. Then all my feares are true, and fhee is falfe;
falfe as a falling Star, or Glow-wormes fire:
This Devill Beautie is compounded ftrangely,
It is a fubtill point, and hard to know,
whether 't has in't more active tempting,
or more paffive tempted; fo foone it forces,
and fo foone it yeelds ———
Good Gods! fhee feiz'd my heart, as if from you
fh'ad had Commiffion to have us'd mee fo;
and all mankinde befides ——— and fee, if the juft Ocean
makes more hafte to pay
to needy rivers, what it borrow'd firft,
then fhee to give, where fhee nere tooke;
mee thinks I feele anger, Revenges harbenger
chalking up all within, and thrufting out
of doores, the tame and fofter paffions; ———
It muft be fo:
To love is noble frailtie, but poore fin

                                     When

When wee fall once to Love, unlov'd agen.   *Exit.*

Enter King, Ariaspes, Jolas.

ARI. 'Twere fit your Juſtice did conſider, (Sir)
what way it tooke ; if you ſhould apprehend
the Prince for Treaſon (which hee never did)
and which, unacted, is unborne ; (at leaſt will be beleev'd ſo)
Iookers on, and the loud talking croud,
will thinke it all but water colours
laid on for a time,
and which wip'd off, each common eye would ſee,
Strange ends, through ſtranger wayes :
    KING. Think'ſt thou I will compound with Treaſon then?
and make one feare anothers Advocate ?
    JOL. Vertue forbid Sir , but if you would permit,
them to approch the roome (yet who would adviſe
Treaſon ſhould come ſo neare ?) there would be then
No place left for excuſe.
    KING. How ſtrong are they ?
    JOL. Weake, conſidering
the enterprize ; they are but few in number,
and thoſe few too, having nothing but
their reſolutions conſiderable about them.
A Troope indeed deſign'd to ſuffer what
they come to execute.
    KING. Who are they are thus wearie of their lives ?
    JOL. Their names I cannot give you.
For thoſe hee ſent for, hee did ſtill receive
at a back doore, and ſo diſmiſt them too.
But I doe thinke *Ziriff* is one.———
    KING. Take heed ! I ſhall ſuſpect thy hate to others,
not thy love to mee, begot this ſervice ;
This Treaſon thou thy ſelfe do'ſt ſay
has but an houres age, and I can give accompt
of him, beyond that time.——— Brother, in the little Tower
where now *Aglaura's* priſoner,
you ſhall finde him ; bring him along,
hee yet doth ſtand untainted in my thoughts,
and to preſerve him ſo,
hee ſhall not ſtirre out of my eyes command
till this great cloud be over.
    JOL. Sir, 'twas the Prince who firſt ———
    KING. I know all that ! urge it no more !
I love the man ;
and 'tis with paine, wee doe ſuſpect,
where wee doe not diſlike :
th'art ſure hee will have ſome,
and that they will come to night ?
    JOL. As ſure as night will come it ſelfe.
    KING. Get all our Guards in readineſſe, we will our ſelfe
diſperſe them afterwards ; and both be ſure
to weare your thoughts within : Ile act the reſt :   *Exeunt.*

Enter Philan, Orſames, *Courtiers.*
    2. COURT. Well.——— If there be not ſome great ſtorme towards,
nere truſt mee ; Whiſper (Court Thunder) is in
everie corner, and there has beene to day
about the Towne a murmuring

and buzzing, such as men ufe to make,
when they doe feare to vent their feares;
    1. COURT. True, and all the Statef-men hang downe their heads,
like full ear'd corne; two of them
where I fup't, ask't what time of night it was,
and when 'twas told them, ftarted, as if
they had beene to run a race.
    2. COURT. The King too (if you marke him,) doth faigne mirth
and jollitie, but through them both,
flafhes of difcontent, and anger make efcapes:
    ORS. Gentlemen! 'tis pittie heav'n
defign'd you not to make the Almanacks.
You gheffe fo fhrewdly by the ill afpects,
or neere conjunctions of the great ones,
at what's to come ftill; that without all doubt
the Countrey had beene govern'd wholly by you,
and plow'd and reap'd accordingly; for mee,
I underftand this myfterie as little
as the new Love, and as I take it too,
'tis much about the Time that everie thing
but Owles, and Lovers take their reft;
Goodnight, *Philan* ——— away —— *Exit.*
    1. COURT. 'Tis early yet; let's goe on the Queens fide
and foole a little; I love to warme my felfe
before I goe to bed, it does beget
handfome and fprightly thoughts, and makes
our dreames halfe folid pleafures.
    2. COURT. Agreed: agreed: *Exeunt.*

ACTUS III. SCENA I.

Enter Prince : Conspiratours :

THER. Couldft thou not finde out *Ziriff?*
    1. COURT. Not fpeake with him my Lord;
yet I fent in by feverall men.
    ORS. I wonder *Iolas* meets us not here too.
    THER. 'Tis ftrange, but let's on now how ere,
when Fortunes, honour, life, and all's in doubt
bravely to dare, is bravely to get out.
        Excursions :   *The Guard upon them.*
    THER. Betrai'd! betrai'd?
    ORS. Shift for your felfe Sir, and let us alone,
wee will fecure your way, and make our owne.   *Exeunt.*
        Enter the King, and Lords.
    KING. Follow Lords, and fee quick execution done,
leave not a man alive.
Who treads on fire, and does not put it out,
Difperfes feare in many fparks of doubt.   *Exeunt.*
        Enter Conspirators, and the Guard upon them.
    ORS. Stand friends, an equall partie ——— (*Fight.*)   *Three of the Conspirators fall,*
    PHI. Brave *Orfames,* 'tis pleafure to dye neere thee. *and three of the Kings fide:*
    ORS. Talke not of dying *Philan,* we will live,   *Orfames and Philan kill*
and ferve the noble Prince agen; we are alone,   *the rest.*
off then with thy difguife, and throw it in the bufhes; *They throw off their disguises.*
                                                    quick,

quick, quick ; before the torrent comes upon us :
wee fhall be ftreight good Subjects, and I defpaire not
of reward for this nights fervice : fo.———
wee two now kill'd our friends ! 'tis hard,
but 'tmuft be fo.

Enter Ariafpes, Jolas, *two Courtiers, part of the Guard.*

A r i. Follow ! Follow !

O r s. Yes ; fo you may now, y'are not likely to overtake.

J o l. *Orfames,* and *Philan,* how came you hither ?

O r s. The neereft way it feemes, you follow'd (thank you)
as if 'thad beene through quickfets :

J o l. 'sDeath have they all efcap'd ?

O r s. Not all, two of them wee made fure ;
but they coft deare, looke here elfe.

A r i. Is the Prince there ?

P h i. They are both Princes I thinke,
they fought like Princes I am fure.   Jolas *puls off the vizors.*

J o l. *Stephines,* and *Odiris* ——— we trifle.
Which way tooke the reft ?

O r s. Two of them are certainly here abouts.

A r i. Upon my life they fwam the river ;
fome ftreight to horfe, and follow ore the bridge ;
you, and I my Lord, will fearch this place a little better.

O r s. Your Highneffe will I hope remember, who were
the men were in———

A r i. Oh ! feare not, your Miftreffe fhall know y'are valiant.

O r s. *Philan!* if thou lov'ft mee, let's kill them upon the place.

P h i. Fie : thou now art wild indeed ;
thou taught'ft mee to be wife firft,
and I will now keepe thee fo. ——— Follow, follow.   *Exeunt.*

Enter Aglaura *with a Lute.*
The Prince comes and knocks within.

T h e r. Madam !

A g l. What wretch is this that thus ufurps
upon the priviledge of Ghofts, and walks
at mid-night ?

T h e r. *Aglaura.*

A g l. Betray mee not
my willing fenfe too foone, yet if that voyce
be falfe. ———

T h e r. Open faire Saint, and let mee in.

A g l. It is the Prince ———
as willingly as thofe
that cannot fleepe doe light ; welcome (Sir,)   (*Opens.*)
welcome above. ———   *Spies his fword drawne.*
Bleffe mee, what meanes this unfheath'd minifter of death?
if, Sir, on mee quick Juftice be to paffe,
why this ? abfence alas, or fuch ftrange lookes
as you now bring with you would kill as foone :

T h e r. Softly ! for I, like a hard hunted Deere,
have only hearded here ; and though the crie
reach not our eares, yet am I follow'd clofe :
ô my heart ! fince I faw thee,
Time has beene ftrangely Active, and begot
a Monftrous iffue of unheard of Storie :
Sit ; thou fhalt have it all ! nay, figh not.

F   fuch

such blasts will hinder all the passage;
Do'st thou remember, how wee parted last?

   AGL. Can I forget it Sir?

   THER. That word of parting was ill plac'd, I sweare,
it may be ominous; but do'st thou know
into whose hands I gave thee?

   AGL. Yes into *Ziriff* Sir.

   THER. That *Ziriff* was thy brother, brave *Zorannes*
preserv'd by miracle in that sad day
thy father fell, and since thus in disguise,
waiting his just revenge.

   AGL. You doe amaze me, Sir.

   THER. And must doe more, when I tell all the Storie.
The King, the jealous King, knew of the marriage,
and when thou thought'st thy selfe by my direction,
thou wert his Prisoner;
unlesse I would renounce all right,
and cease to love thee, (ô strange, and fond request!)
immur'd thou must have beene in some sad place,
and lockt for ever, from *Thersames* sight.
For ever ———— and that unable to indure
this night, I did attempt his life.

   AGL. Was it well done Sir?

   THER. O no! extremely Ill!
for to attempt and not to act was poore:
here the dead-doing Law, (like ill-paid Souldiers)
leaves the side 'twas on, to joyne with power.
Royall villany now will looke so like to Justice,
that the times to come and curious posteritie,
will finde no difference: weep'st thou *Aglaura?*
come, to bed my Love!
and wee will there mock Tyrannie, and Fate,
those softer houres of pleasure, and delight,
that like so many single pearles, should have
adorn'd our thread of life, wee will at once,
by Loves mysterious power, and this nights help
contract to one, and make but one rich draught
of all.

   AGL. What meane you Sir?

   THER. To make my selfe incapable of miserie,
by taking strong preservative of happinesse:
I would this night injoy thee:

   AGL. Doe: Sir, doe what you will with mee,
for I am too much yours, to deny the right
how ever claim'd ——— but ———

   THER. But what *Aglaura?*

   AGL. Gather not roses in a wet and frowing houre,
they'll lose their sweets then, trust mee they will Sir.
What pleasure can Love take to play his game out,
when death must keepe the Stakes ——— *A noise without.*
harke Sir ——— grave bringers, and last minutes are at hand,
hide, hide your selfe, for Loves sake hide your selfe.

   THER. As soone the Sunne may hide himselfe, as I.
The Prince of *Persia* hide himselfe? ———

   AGL. O talke not Sir; the Sunne does hide himselfe
when night and blacknesse comes ———

THER.

THER. Never sweet Ignorance, he shines in th'other world then;
and so shall I, if I set here in glorie :

Enter   *Opens the doore, enter* Ziriff.
yee hastie seekers of life.
Sorannez. ———

AGL. My brother!
If all the joy within mee come not out,
to give a welcome to so deare an object,
excuse it Sir ; sorrow locks up all doores.

ZIR. If there be such a Toy about you, Sister,
keep't for your selfe, or lend it to the Prince ;
there is a dearth of that Commoditie,
and you have made it Sir. Now ?
what is the next mad thing you meane to doe ?
will you stay here ? when all the Court's beset
like to a wood at a great hunt, and busie mischiefe hastes
to be in view, and have you in her power ———

THER. To mee all this ———
for great griefe's deafe as well as it is dumbe,
and drives no trade at all with Counsell : (Sir)
why doe you not Tutor one that has the Plague,
and see if hee will feare an after ague fit ;
such is all mischiefe now to mee ; there is none left
is worth a thought, death is the worst, I know,
and that compar'd to shame, does looke more lovely now
than a chaste Mistresse, set by common woman ———
and I must court it Sir ?

ZIR. No wonder if that heav'n forsake us, when wee leave our selves :
what is there done should feed such high despaire ?
were you but safe ———

AGL. Deare (Sir) be rul'd,
if love, be love, and magick too,
(as sure it is where it is true ;)
wee then shall meet in absence, and in spight
of all divorce, freely enjoy together,
what niggard Fate thus peevishly denies.

THER. Yea : but if pleasures be themselves but dreames,
what then are the dreames of these to men ?
that monster, Expectation, will devoure
all that is within our hope or power,
and ere wee once can come to shew, how rich
wee are, wee shall be poore,
shall wee not *Sorannez* ?

ZIR. I understand not this,
in times of envious penurie (such as these are)
to keepe but love alive is faire, wee should not thinke
of feasting him : come (Sir)
here in these lodgings is a little doore,
that leads unto another ; that againe,
unto a vault, that has his passage under
the little river, opening into the wood ;
from thence 'tis but some few minutes easie businesse
unto a Servants house of mine (who for his faith
and honestie, hereafter must
looke big in Storie) there you are safe however ;
and when this Storme has met a little calme,

what wild defire dares whifper to it felfe,
you may enjoy, and at the worft may fteale :
   THER.   What fhall become of thee *Aglaura* then ?
fhall I leave thee their rages facrifice ?
and like dull Sea-men threatned with a ftorme,
throw all away, I have, to fave my felfe.
   AGL.   Can I be fafe when you are not ? my Lord !
knowes love in us divided happineffe ?
am I the fafer for your being here ?
can you give that you have not for your felfe ?
my innocence is my beft guard, and that your ftay
betraying it unto fufpition, takes away.
If you did love mee ? ———
   THER.   Growes that in queftion ? then 'tis time to part : ——— *Kiffes her.*
when wee fhall meet againe *Heav'n* onely knowes,
and when wee fhall I know we fhall be old:
Love does not calculate the common way,
Minutes are houres there, and the houres are dayes,
each day's a yeare, and everie yeare an age;
what will this come to thinke you ?
   ZIR.   Would this were all the ill,
for thefe are prettie little harmleffe nothings;
Times horfe runs full as faft, hard borne and curb'd,
as in his full carreere, loofe-rain'd and fpurr'd:
come, come, let's away.
   THER.   Happineffe, fuch as men loft in miferie
would wrong in naming, 'tis fo much above them.
All that I want of it, all you deferve,
Heav'n fend you in my abfence.
   AGL.   And miferie, fuch as wittie malice would
lay out in curfes, on the thing it hates,
Heav'n fend mee in the ftead, if when y'are gone
I welcome it, but for your fake alone. ——— *Exeunt.*   *Leads him out, and en-*
   ZIR.   Stir not from hence, Sir, till you heare from me *ters up out of the vault.*
fo goodnight deere Prince.
   THER.   Goodnight deere friend.
   ZIR.   When wee meet next all this will but advance ——
Joy never feafts fo high,
as when the firft courfe is of miferie.   *Exeunt.*

ACTUS IV. SCENA I.

Enter three or foure Courtiers.

   1. COURT. BY this light ——— a brave Prince,
hee made no more of the Guard, than they would of a Taylor on
a Maske night, that has refus'd trufting before.
   2. COURT.   Hee's as Active as he is valiant too;
did'ft mark him how hee ftood like all the points
o'th' Compaffe, and as good Pictures,
had his eyes, towards everie man.
   3. COURT.   And his fword too,
all th'other fide walk up and downe the Court now,
as if they had loft their way, and ftare,
like Grey-hounds, when the Hare has taken the furze.

           1. COURT.

1. COURT. Right,
and have more troubles about'em
than a Serving-man that has forgot his meſſage
when hee's come upon the place. ————
    2. COURT. Yonder's the King within, chafing, and ſwearing
like an old Falconer upon the firſt flight
of a young Hawke, when ſome Clowne
has taken away the quarrie from her ;
and all the Lords ſtand round about him,
as if hee were to be baited, with much more feare,
and at much more diſtance,
than a Countrey Gentlewoman ſees the Lions the firſt time :
looke : hee's broke looſe. ————

Enter King and Lords.

KING. Finde him ; or by *Oſiris* ſelfe, you all are Traitours ;
and equally ſhall pay to Juſtice ; a ſingle man,
and guiltie too, breake through you all !

Enter Ziriff.

ZIR. Confidence !
(thou paint of women, and the Stateſ-mans wiſdome,
valour for Cowards, and of the guilties Innocence,)
aſſiſt mee now.
Sir, ſend theſe Starers off :
I have ſome buſineſſe will deſerve your privacie.

KING. Leave us.

JOL. How the villaine ſwells vpon us ?—— *Exeunt.*

ZIR. Not to puniſh thought,
or keepe it long upon the wrack of doubt,
know Sir,
That by corruption of the waiting woman,
the common key of Secrets; I have found
the truth at laſt, and have diſcover'd all :
the Prince your Sonne was by *Aglaura's* meanes,
convey'd laſt night unto the Cypreſſe Grove,
through a cloſe vault that opens in the lodgings :
hee does intend to joyne with *Carimania*,
but ere hee goes, reſolves to finiſh all
the rites of Love, and this night meanes
to ſteale what is behinde.

KING. How good is Heav'n unto mee !
that when it gave mee Traitours for my Subjects,
would lend mee ſuch a Servant !

ZIR. How juſt (Sir) rather,
that would beſtow this Fortune on the poore.
and where your bountie had made debt ſo infinite
that it grew deſperate, their hope to pay it————

KING. Enough of that, thou do'ſt but gently chide
mee for a fault, that I will mend ; for I
have beene too poore, and low in my rewards
unto thy vertue : but to our buſineſſe ;
the queſtion is, whether wee ſhall rely
upon our Guards agen ?

ZIR. By no meanes Sir :
hope on his future fortunes, or their Love
unto his perſon, has ſo ſicklied ore
their reſolutions, that wee muſt not
truſt them.   G   Beſides,

Besides, it were but needlesse here;
hee passes through the vault alone, and I
my selfe durst undertake that businesse,
if that were all, but there is something else,
this accident doth prompt my zeale to serve you in.
I know you love *Aglaura* (Sir) with passion,
and would enjoy her; I know besides
shee loves him so, that whosoere shall bring
the tidings of his death, must carrie back
the newes of hers, so that your Justice (Sir)
must rob your hope: but there is yet a way——

    KING. Here! take my heart; for I have hitherto
too vainly spent the treasure of my love,
Ile have it coyn'd streight into friendship all,
and make a present to thee.

    ZIR. If any part of this rich happinesse,
(Fortune prepares now for you) shall owe it selfe
unto my weake endevours, I have enough.
Aglaura without doubt this night expects
the Prince, and why
you should not then supply his place by stealth,
and in disguise——

    KING. I apprehend thee *Ziriff*,
but there's difficultie ——

    ZIR. Who trades in Love must be an adventurer, (Sir)
but here is scarce enough to make the pleasure dearer:
I know the Cave; your Brother and my selfe
with *Iolas*, (for those w'are sure doe hate him,)
with some few chosen more betimes will wait
the Princes passing through the vault; if hee
comes first, hee's dead; and if it be your selfe,
wee will conduct you to the chamber doore,
and stand 'twixt you and danger afterwards.

    KING. I have conceiv'd of Joy, and am growne great:
Till I have safe deliverance, time's a cripple
and goes on crutches. —— as for thee my *Ziriff*,
I doe here entertaine a friendship with thee,
shall drowne the memorie of all patternes past;
wee will oblige by turnes; and that so thick,
and fast, that curious studiers of it,
shall not once dare to cast it up, or say
by way of ghesse, whether thou or I
remaine the debtors, when wee come to die.   *Exeunt.*

      Enter Semanthe, Orithie, Philan, Orsames, *Lords and Ladies.*

    ORI. Is the Queene ready to come out?
    PHI. Not yet sure, the Kings brother is but newly entred;
    SEM. Come my Lord, the Song then.
    ORI. The Song.
    ORS. A vengeance take this love, it spoyles a voyce
worse than the losing of a maiden-head.
I have got such a cold with rising
and walking in my shirt a nights, that
a Bittorne whooping in a reed is better musike.
    ORI. This modestie becomes you as ill, my Lord,
as wooing would us women; pray, put's not to't.
    ORS. Nay Ladies, you shall finde mee,

as free, as the Muficians of the woods
themfelves; what I have, you fhall not need to call for,
nor fhall it coft you any thing.

SONG.

Why fo pale and wan fond Lover?
      Prithee why fo pale?
Will, when looking well can't moue her,
      Looking ill prevaile?
      Prithee why fo pale?

Why fo dull and mute young Sinner?
      Prithee why fo mute?
Will, when fpeaking well can't win her,
      Saying nothing doo't?
      Prithee why fo mute?

Quit, quit, for fhame, this will not moue
      This cannot take her,
If of her felfe fhee will not Loue,
      Nothing can make her,
      The Deuill take her.

ORI. I fhould haue gheft, it had been the iffue of
your braine, if I had not beene told fo;
ORS. A little foolifh counfell (Madam) I gaue a friend
of mine foure or fiue yeares agoe, when he was
falling into a Confumption. ——

Enter Queene.

ORB. Which of all you haue feene the faire prifoner
fince fhee was confinde?
SEM. I haue Madam.
ORB. And how behaues fhee now her felfe?
SEM. As one that had intrench'd fo deepe in Innocence,
fhee fear'd no enemies, beares all quietly,
and fmiles at Fortune, whil'ft fhee frownes on her.
ORB. So gallant! I wonder where the beautie lies
that thus inflames the royall bloud?
ORI. Faces, Madam, are like bookes, thofe that doe ftudy them
know beft, and to fay truth, 'tis ftill
much as it pleafes the Courteous Reader.
ORB. Thefe Louers fure are like Aftronomers,
that when the vulgar eye difcouers, but
a Skie aboue, ftudded with fome few Stars,
finde out befides ftrange fifhes, birds, and beafts.
SEM. As men in ficknefle fcortch'd into a rauing
doe fee the Deuill, in all fhapes and formes,
when ftanders by wondring, aske where, and when;
So they in Loue, for all's but feauer there,
and madnefle too.
ORB. That's too feuere Semanthe;
but wee will haue your reafons in the parke;
are the doores open through the Gardens?
LO. The King has newly led the way.   *Exeunt.*

Enter Ariafpes: Ziriff, with a warrant fealed.
ARI. Thou art a Tyrant, Ziriff: I fhall die with joy.

Zir.

ZIR. I must confesse my Lord; had but the Princes ills
prov'd sleight, and not thus dangerous,
hee should have ow'd to mee, at least I would
have laid a claime unto his safetie; and
like Physicians, that doe challenge right
in Natures cures, look'd for reward and thanks;
but since 'twas otherwise, I thought it best
to save my selfe, and then to save the State.

ARI. 'Twas wisely done.

ZIR. Safely I'me sure, my Lord! you know 'tis not
our custome, where the Kings dislike, once swells to hate,
there to ingage our selves; Court friendship
is a Cable, that in stormes is ever cut,
and I made bold with it; here is the warrant seal'd
and for the execution of it, if you thinke
wee are not strong enough, wee may have
Iolas, for him the King did name.

ARI. And him I would have named.

ZIR. But is hee not too much the Prince's (Sir?)

ARI. Hee is as lights in Scenes at Masques,
what glorious shew so ere hee makes without,
I that set him there, know why, and how;   *Enter* Jolas.
but here hee is. ———
Come *Iolas;* and since the Heav'ns decreed,
the man whom thou should'st envie, should be such,
That all men else must doo't; be not asham'd
thou once wert guiltie of it;
but blesse them, that they give thee now a meanes,
to make a friendship with him, and vouchsafe
to finde thee out a way to love, where well
thou could'st not hate.

JOL. What meanes my Lord?

ARI. Here, here hee stands that has preserv'd us all!
that sacrifis'd unto a publique good,
(the dearest private good wee mortalls have)
Friendship: gave into our armes the Prince,
when nothing but the sword (perchance a ruine)
was left to doe it.

JOL. How could I chide my love, and my ambition now,
that thrust mee upon such a quarrell? here I doe vow ——

ZIR. Hold, doe not vow my Lord, let it deserve it first;
and yet (if Heav'n blesse honest mens intents)
'tis not impossible.
My Lord, you will be pleas'd to informe him in particulars,
I must be gone. ———
the King I feare already has beene left
too long alone.

ARI. Stay ——— the houre and place.

ZIR. Eleven, under the Tarras walke;
I will not faile you there.   *Goes out, returnes back againe.*
I had forgot: ———
'tmay be, the small remainder of those lost men
that were of the Conspiracie, will come along with him:
'twere best to have some chosen of the Guard
within our call ———   *Exit* Ziriff.

ARI. Honest, and carefull *Ziriff:*   Jolas *stands musing.*

how

how now Planet ſtrooke ? ——

JoL. This *Z1riff* will grow great with all the world.

ARI. Shallow man ! ſhort ſightedder than Travellers in miſts,
or women that outlive themſelves ; do'ſt thou not ſee,
that whil'ſt hee does prepare a Tombe with one hand
for his friend, hee digs a Grave with th'other for himſelfe?

JoL. How ſo ?

ARI. Do'ſt thinke hee ſhall not feele the weight of this,
as well as poore *Therſames* ?

JoL. Shall wee then kill him too at the ſame inſtant ?

ARI. And ſay, the Prince made an unluckie thruſt.

JoL. Right.

ARI. Dull, dull, hee muſt not dye ſo uſeleſly.
As when wee wipe of filth from any place,
wee throw away the thing that made it cleane,
ſo this once done, hee's gone.
Thou know'ſt the People love the Prince, to their rage
ſomething the State muſt offer up ; who fitter
than thy rivall and my enemy ?

JoL. Rare ! our witneſſe will be taken.

ARI. Piſh ! let mee alone.
The Grants that made mountaines ladders,
and thought to take great *Iov* by force, were fooles :
not hill on hill, but plot on plot, does make
us ſit above, and laugh at all below us. —— *Exeunt.*

Enter Aglaura, *and a Singing Boy.*

BOY. Madam, 'twill make you melancholly,
Ile ſing the *Prince's* Song, that's ſad enough.

AGL. What you will Sir.

SONG.

NO, no, *faire Heretique, it needs muſt bee*
   But an ill Love in mee,
   And worſe for thee.

For were it in my Power,
To love thee now this hower,
   More than I did the laſt ;

I would then ſo faſt,
   I might not Love at all ;

Love that can flow, and can admit increaſe,
Admits as well an Ebb, and may grow leſſe.

2

True Love is ſtill the ſame ; the torrid Zones,
   And thoſe more frigid ones,
   It muſt not know :

For Love growne cold or hot,
   Is Luſt, or Friendſhip, not
   The thing wee have ;

For that's a flame would die,
Held downe, or up to high :

  Then thinke I love more than I can expreſſe,
  And would love more, could I but love thee leſſe.

H

AGL. Leave mee! for to a Soule, so out of Tune
as mine is now ; nothing is harmony :
when once the maine-spring, *Hope,* is falne into
disorder ; no wonder, if the lesser wheeles,
Desire, and *Ioy,* stand still; my thoughts like *Bees*
when they have lost their King, wander
confusedly up and downe, and settle no where.

Enter Orithie.

Orithie, flie ! flie the roome,
as thou would'st shun the habitations
which Spirits haunt, or where thy nearer friends
walk after death ; here is not only Love,
but Loves plague too —— mis-fortune ; and so high,
that it is sure infectious !

ORI. Madam, so much more miserable am I this way than you,
that should I pitie you, I should forget my selfe :
my sufferings are such, that with lesse patience
you may endure your owne, than give mine Audience.
There is that difference, that you may make
yours none at all, but by considering mine !

AGL. O speake them quickly then ! the marriage day
to passionate Lovers never was more welcome,
than any kinde of ease would be to mee now.

ORI. Could they be spoke, they were not then so great.
I love, and dare not say I love ; dare not hope,
what I desire ; yet still too must desire ——
and like a starving man brought to a feast,
and made say grace, to what he nere shall taste,
be thankfull after all, and kisse the hand,
that made the wound thus deepe.

AGL. 'Tis hard indeed, but with what unjust scales,
thou took'st the weight of our mis-fortunes,
be thine owne Judge now.
thou mourn'st for losse of that thou never hadst,
or if thou hadst a losse, it never was
of a *Thersames.*
would'st thou not thinke a Merchant mad, *Orithie* ?
if thou shouldst see him weepe, and teare his haire,
because hee brought not both the Indies home ?
and wouldst not thinke his sorrowes verie just,
if having fraught his ship with some rich Treasure,
hee sunke i'th' verie Port ? This is our case.

ORI. And doe you thinke there is such odds in it ?
would Heaven we women could as easily change
our fortunes as ('tis said) wee can our minds.
I cannot (Madam) thinke them miserable,
that have the Princes Love.

AGL. Hee is the man then ——
blush not *Orithie,* 'tis a sinne to blush
for loving him, though none at all to love him.
I can admit of rivalship without
a jealousie —— nay shall be glad of it :
wee two will sit, and thinke, and thinke, and sigh,
and sigh, and talke of love —— and of *Thersames.*
Thou shalt be praising of his wit, while I
admire he governes it so well :

like this thing, said thus, th'other thing thus done,
and in good language him for these adore,
while I want words to doo't, yet doe it more.
Thus will wee doe, till death it selfe shall us
divide, and then whose fate 'tshall be to die
first of the two, by legacie shall all
her love bequeath, and give her stock to her
that shall survive; for no one stock can serve,
to love *Thersames* so as hee'll deserve.

Enter King, Ziriff.

KING. What have wee here impossibilitie?
a constant night, and yet within the roome
that, that can make the day before the Sunne?
silent *Aglaura* too?

AGL. I know not what to say:
Is't to your pitie, or your scorne, I owe
the favour of this visit (Sir?) for such
my fortune is, it doth deserve them both:

KING. And such thy beautie is, that it makes good
all Fortunes, sorrow lookes lovely here;
and there's no man, that would not entertaine
his griefes as friends, were hee but sure they'd shew
no worse upon him —— but I forget my selfe,
I came to chide.

AGL. If I have sinn'd so high, that yet my punishment
equalls not my crime,
doe Sir; I should be loth to die in debt
to Justice, how ill soere I paid
the scores of Love. ——

KING. And those indeed thou hast but paid indifferently
to mee, I did deserve at least faire death,
not to be murthered thus in private:
that was too cruell, Mistresse.
And I doe know thou do'st repent, and wilt
yet make mee satisfaction:

AGL. What satisfaction Sir?
I am no monster, never had two hearts;
One is by holy vowes anothers now,
and could I give it you, you would not take it,
for'tis alike impossible for mee,
to love againe, as you love Perjurie.
O Sir! consider, what a flame love is.
If by rude meanes you thinke to force a light,
that of it selfe it would not freely give,
you blow it out, and leave your selfe i'th' darke.
The Prince once gone, you may as well perswade
the light to stay behinde, when the Sun posts
to th'other world, as mee; alas! wee two,
have mingled soules more than two meeting brooks;
and whosoever is design'd to be
the murtherer of my Lord; (as sure there is,
has anger'd heav'n so farre, that 'tas decreed
him to encrease his punishment that way)
would hee but search the heart, when hee has done,
hee there would finde *Aglaura* murther'd too.

KING. Thou hast orecome mee, mov'd so handsomely

for pitie, that I will dif-inherit
the elder brother, and from this houre be
thy Convert, not thy Lover. ———
Ziriff, difpatch away ———
and hee that brings newes of the Prince's welfare,
looke that hee have the fame reward, wee had decreed
to him, brought tidings of his death.
'Tmuft be a bufie and bold hand, that would
unlinke a chaine the Gods themfelves have made :
peace to thy Thoughts : *Aglaura* ——— *Exit.*

> *Ziriff fteps back and fpeakes.*

ZIR. What ere he fayes beleeve him not *Aglaura*:
for luft and rage ride high within him now :
hee knowes *Therfames* made th'efcape from hence,
and does conceale it only for his ends :
for by the favour of miftake and night,
hee hopes t'enjoy thee in the Prince's roome ;
I fhall be mift ——— elfe I would tell thee more ;
But thou mayeft gheffe, for our condition
admits no middle wayes, either wee muft
fend them to Graves, or lie our felves in duft:——*Exit.*

> *Aglaura ftands ftill and ftudies.*

AGL. Ha! 'tis a ftrange Act thought puts me now upon;
yet fure my brother meant the felfe fame thing,
and my *Therfames* would have done't for mee :
to take his life, that feekes to take away
the life of Life, (honour from mee ;) and from
the world, the life of honour, *Therfames*;
muft needs be fomething fure, of kin to Juftice.
If I doe faile, th'attempt howere was brave,
and I fhall have at worft a handfome grave——— *Exit.*

> *Enter* Jolas, Semanthe.
> Semanthe *fteps back,* Jolas *ftayes her.*

JOL. What ? are we growne, *Semanthe,* night, and day ?
Muft one ftill vanifh when the other comes ?
Of all that ever Love did yet bring forth
(and 't has beene fruitfull too,) this is
the ftrangeft Iffue. ——

SEM. What my Lord ?

JOL. Hate, *Semanthe.*

SEM. You doe miftake, if I doe fhun you, 'tis,
as bafhfull Debtors fhun their Creditors,
I cannot pay you in the felfe fame coyne,
and am afham'd to offer any other.

JOL. It is ill done, *Semanthe,* to plead bankrupt,
when with fuch eafe you may be out of debt;
In loves dominions, native commoditie
is currant payment, change is all the Trade,
and heart for heart, the richeft merchandize.

SEM. 'Twould here be meane my Lord, fince mine would prove
In your hands but a Counterfeit, and yours in mine
worth nothing ; Sympathy, not greatneffe,
makes thofe Jewells rife in value.

JOL. Sympathy ! ô teach but yours to love then,
and two fo rich no mortall ever knew.

SEM. That heart would Love but ill that muft be taught,

fuch

such fires as these still kindle of themselves.

Jol. In such a cold, and frozen place, as is
thy breast? how should they kindle of themselves
Semanthe?

Sem. Aske? how the Flint can carrie fire within?
'tis the least miracle that Love can doe:

Jol. Thou art thy selfe the greatest miracle,
for thou art faire to all perfection,
and yet do'st want the greatest part of beautie,
Kindnesse; thy crueltie (next to thy selfe,)
above all things on earth takes up my wonder.

Sem. Call not that crueltie, which is our fate,
beleeve me *Iolas*, the honest Swaine
that from the brow of some steepe cliffe far off,
beholds a ship labouring in vaine against
the boysterous and unruly Elements, ne're had
lesse power, or more desire to help than I;
at everie sigh, I die, and everie looke,
does move; and any passion you will have
but Love, I have in store: I will be angrie,
quarrell with destinie, and with my selfe
that 'tis no better; be melancholy;
And (though mine owne disasters well might plead
to be in chiefe,) yours only shall have place,
Ile pitie, and (if that's too low) Ile grieve,
as for my sinnes, I cannot give you ease;
all this I doe, and this I hope will prove
'tis greater Torment not to love, than Love. —— *Exit.*

Jol. So perishing Sailours pray to stormes,
and so they heare agen. So men
with death about them, looke on Physitians that
have given them o're, and so they turne away:
Two fixed Stars that keepe a constant distance,
and by lawes made with themselves must know
no motion excentrick, may meet as soone as wee:
The anger that the foolish Sea does shew,
when it does brave it out, and rore against
a stubborne rock that still denies it passage,
is not so vaine and fruitlesse, as my prayers.
Yee mightie Powers of Love and Fate, where is
your Justice here? It is thy part (fond Boy)
when thou do'st finde one wounded heart, to make
the other so, but if thy Tyranny
be such, that thou wilt leave one breast to hate,
If wee must live, and this survive,
how much more cruell's Fate? ——— *Exit.*

Actus V. Scena I.

Enter Ziriff, Ariaspes, Jolas.

Jol. A Glorious night!
     Ari. Pray Heav'n it prove so.
Are wee not there yet?
   Zir. 'Tis about this hollow.   *Enter the Cave.*

I

ARI. How now ! what region are we got into ?
Th'enheritance of night ;
Are wee not miftaken a turning *Ziriff,*
and ftept into fome melancholy Devils Territorie ?
Sure 'tis a part of the firft *Chaos,*
that would endure no change.

ZIR. No matter Sir, 'tis as proper for our purpofe,
as the Lobbie for the waiting womans.
Stay you here, Ile move a little backward,
and fo wee fhall be fure to put him paft
retreat : you know the word if't be the Prince.   *Goes to the mouth of the Cave.*

Enter King.

Here Sir, follow mee, all's quiet yet. ——

KING. Hee is not come then ?

ZIR. No.

KING. Where's *Ariafpes* ?

ZIR. Waiting within.   *Hee leads him on, fteps behinde him,*

JOL. I doe not like this waiting,   *gives the false word, they kill the*
nor this fellowes leaving us.   *King.*

ARI. This place does put odd thoughts into thee,
then thou art in thine owne nature too, as jealous
as either Love, or Honor : Come, weare thy fword in readines,
and thinke how neere wee are a crowne.

ZIR. Revenge !
So let's drag him to the light, and fearch
his pockets, there may be papers there that will
difcover the reft of the Confpiratours.
Iolas, your hand ——   *Draw him out.*

JOL. Whom have wee here ? the King !

ZIR. Yes, and *Zorrannes* too, Illo ! hoe ! —— *Enter Pafithas and others.*
Unarme them.
D'ee ftare ?
This for my Fathers injuries and mine :   *Points to the Kings dead body.*
halfe Love, halfe Duties Sacrifice,
this —— for the noble Prince, an offering to friendfhip :   *Runs at Jolas.*

JOL. Bafely ! and tamely ———   *Dies.*

ARI. What haft thou done ?

ZIR. Nothing —— kill'd a Traytour,
So —— away with them, and leaves us,
Pafithas be onely you in call.

ARI. What do'ft thou pawfe ?
haft thou remorfe already murtherer ?

ZIR. No foole : 'tis but a difference I put
betwixt the crimes : *Orbella* is our quarrell ;
and I doe hold it fit, that love fhould have
a nobler way of Juftice, than Revenge
or Treafon ; follow mee out of the wood,
and thou fhalt be Mafter of this againe :
and then, beft arme and title take it.   *They goe out and enter agen.*
There ——   *Gives him his fword.*

ARI. Extremely good ! Nature tooke paines I fweare,
the villaine and the brave are mingled handfomly.

ZIR. 'Twas Fate that tooke it, when it decreed
wee two fhould meet, nor fhall they mingle now
wee are brought together ftrait to part. ——   *Fight,*

ARI. Some Devill fure has borrowed this fhape.   *Pawfe.*

my sword ne're stay'd thus long to finde an entrance.

ZIR. To guiltie men, all that appeares is Devill,
come Trifler, come. ——— *Fight againe,* Ariaspes *falls.*

ARI. Whither, whither, thou fleeting Coward life?
Bubble of Time, Natures shame, stay; a little, stay!
till I have look'd my selfe into revenge,
and star'd this Traytour to a carcasse first.

——— It will not be: ——— *Falls.*
the Crowne, the Crowne, too
now is lost, for ever lost ——— oh! ———
Ambition's, but an *Ignis fatuus,* I see
misleading fond mortalitie,
That hurries us about, and sets us downe
Just ——— where—— wee—— first—— begun ——— *Dies.*

ZIR. What a great spreading mightie thing this was,
and what a nothing now? how soone poore man
vanishes into his noone-tide shadow?
but hopes o're fed have seldome better done: —— *(Hollowes.)* Enter Pasithas.
Take up this lump of vanitie, and honour,
and carrie it the back way to my lodging,
there may be use of Statef-men, when th'are dead:
So. ——— for the Cittadell now, for in such times
as these, when the unruly multitude
is up in swarmes, and no man knowes which way
they'll take, 'tis good to have retreat. *Exeunt.*

Enter Thersames.

THER. The Dog-star's got up high, it should be late:
and sure by this time everie waking care,
and watchfull eye is charm'd; and yet mee thought
a noyse of weapons strucke my eare just now.
'Twas but my Fancie sure, and were it more,
I would not tread one step, that did not lead
to my *Aglavra,* stood all his Guard betwixt,
with lightning in their hands;
Danger! thou Dwarfe drest up in Giants clothes,
that shew'st farre off, still greater than thou art:
goe, terrifie the simple, and the guiltie, such
as with false Opticks, still doe looke upon thee.
But fright not Lovers; wee dare looke on thee
in thy worst shape, and meet thee in them too.
Stay —— These trees I made my marke, 'tis hereabouts,
——— Love guide mee but right this night,
and Lovers shall restore thee back againe
those eyes the Poets tooke so boldly from thee. *Exit.*

Aglaura *with a torch in one hand, and a dagger in the other.*

AGL. How ill this does become this hand, how much worse
this suits with this, one of the two should goe.
The shee within mee sayes, it must be this ———
honour sayes this ——— and honour is *Thersames* friend.
What is that shee then? it is not a thing
that sets a Price, not upon mee, but on
life in my name, leading mee into doubt,
which when 'tas done, it cannot light mee out.
For feare does drive to Fate, or Fate if wee
doe flie, oretakes, and holds us, till or death,
or infamie, or both doth cease us. ——— *Puts out the light.*

Ha! —— would 'twere in agen.
Antiques and strange mishapes,
such as the Porter to my Soule, mine Eye,
was ne're acquainted with, Fancie lets in,
like a distracted multitude, by some strange accident
piec'd together, feare now afresh comes on,
and charges Love to home.
—— Hee comes —— hee comes ——
woman, if thou would'st be the Subject of mans wonder, not his scorne hereafter,
now shew thy selfe.

Enter Prince rising from the vault, shee stabs him two or three times, hee falls, shees goes back to her chamber.

Sudden and fortunate.
My better Angell sure did both infuse
a strength, and did direct it. *Enter* Ziriff.

   ZIR. *Aglaura!*
   AGL. Brother ——
   ZIR. The same.
So slow to let in such a long'd for Guest?
must Joy stand knocking Sister, come, prepare,
prepare. ——
The King of *Persia*'s comming to you strait!
the King! —— marke that.
   AGL. I thought how poore the Joyes you brought with you,
were in respect of those that were with mee:
Joyes, are our hopes stript of their feares,
and such are mine; for know, deare Brother,
the King is come already, and is gone —— marke that.
   ZIR. Is this instinct, or riddle? what King? how gone?
   AGL. The Cave will tell you more ——
   ZIR. Some sad mistake —— thou hast undone us all. *Goes out, enters hastily againe.*
The Prince! the Prince! cold as the bed of earth
hee lies upon, as senslesse too; death hangs
upon his lips,
like an untimely frost, upon an early Cherrie;
the noble Guest, his Soule, tooke it so ill
that you should use his old Acquaintance so,
that neither pray'rs, nor teares, can e're perswade
him back againe. —— *Aglaura swounes: rubs her.*
hold, hold! wee cannot sure part thus!
Sister! *Aglaura! Thersames* is not dead,
It is the Prince that calls ——
   AGL. The Prince, where? ——
Tell mee, or I will strait goe back againe,
into those groves of Gessemine, thou took'st mee from,
and finde him out, or lose my selfe for ever.
   ZIR. For ever. —— I: there's it!
for in those groves thou talk'st of,
there are so many by-wayes, and odd turnings,
leading unto such wild and dismall places,
that should wee goe without a guide, or stir
before Heav'n calls, 'tis strongly to be feared
wee there should wander up and downe for ever,
and be benighted to eternitie! ——
   AGL. Benighted to eternitie? —— What's that?
   ZIR. Why 'tis to be benighted to eternitie;

to fit i'th' darke, and doe I know not what;
unriddle at our owne fad coft and charge,
the doubts the learned here doe onely move. ————

AGL. What place have murtherers brother there? for fure
the murtherer of the Prince muft have
a punifhment that Heaven is yet to make. ————

ZIR. How is religion fool'd betwixt our loves,
and feares? poore Girle, for ought that thou haft done,
thy Chaplets may be faire and flourifhing,
as his in the *Elyfium* :

AGL. Doe you thinke fo?

ZIR. Yes, I doe thinke fo.
The jufter Judges of our Actions,
would they have beene fevere upon
our weakneffes,
would (fure) have made us ftronger. ————
Fie ! thofe teares
a Bride upon the marriage day as properly
might fhed as thou, here widowes doo't
and marrie next day after :
To fuch a funerall as this, there fhould be
nothing common ————
Wee'll mourne him fo, that thofe that are alive
fhall thinke themfelves more buried far than hee;
and wifh to have his grave, to finde his Obfequies :
but ftay ———— the Body. *Brings up the bodie, fhee fwounes and dies.*
Agen ! Sifter ———— *Aglaura* ————
ô fpeake once more, once more looke out faire Soule. ————
Shee's gone. ————
Irrevocably gone. ———— And winging now the Aire,
like a glad bird broken from fome cage :
poore Bankrupt heart, when 'thad not wherewithall
to pay to fad difafter all that was its due,
it broke ———— would mine would doe fo too.
My foule is now within mee
like a well metled Hauke, on a blinde Faulk'ners fift,
mee thinks I feele it baiting to be gone :
and yet I have a little foolifh bufineffe here
on earth; I will difpatch : ———— *Exit.*

Enter Pafithas, *with the body of* Ariafpes.

PAS. Let mee bee like my burthen here, if I had not as lieve kill two of the
Bloud-royall for him, as carrie one of them; Thefe Gentlemen of high actions are
three times as heavie after death, as your private retir'd ones; looke if hee be not re-
duc'd to the ftate of a Courtier of the fecond forme now? and cannot ftand upon
his 'owne legs, nor doe any thing without help, Hum. ———— And what's become
of the great Prince, in prifon as they call it now, the toy within us, that makes us
talke, and laugh, and fight, I! why there's it, well, let him be what hee will, and
where hee will, Ile make bold with the old Tenement here. Come Sir ———— come
along : ———— *Exit.*

Enter Ziriff.

ZIR. All's faft too, here ————
They fleepe to night
i'their winding fheets I thinke, there's fuch
a generall quiet.
Oh ! here's light I warrant :
for luft does take as little reft, as care, or age. ————

K   Courting

Courting her glaſſe, I ſweare, fie ! that's a flatterer Madam,
in mee you ſhall ſee trulier what you are.   *Knocks.*   *Enter the Queene.*

   Orb. What make you up at this ſtrange houre my Lord ?

   Zir. My buſineſſe is my boldneſſe warrant,
(Madam)
and I could well afford t'have beene without it now,
had Heav'n ſo pleas'd,

   Orb. 'Tis a ſad Prologue,
what followes in the name of vertue ?

   Zir. The King.

   Orb. I : what of him ? is well is hee not ?

   Zir. Yes. ――――
If to be free from the great load
wee ſweat and labour under, here on earth
be to be well, hee is.

   Orb. Why hee's not dead, is hee ?

   Zir. Yes Madam, ſlaine ―― and the Prince too.

   Orb. How ? where ?

   Zir. I know not, but dead they are.

   Orb. Dead !

   Zir. Yes Madam.

   Orb. Didſt ſee them dead ?

   Zir. As I ſee you alive.

   Orb. Dead !

   Zir. Yes, dead.

   Orb. Well, wee muſt all die ;
the Siſters ſpin no cables for us mortalls ;
th'are thred ; and Time, and chance――――
truſt mee I could weep now,
but watrie diſtillations doe but ill on graves,
they make the lodging colder.   *Shee knocks.*

   Zir. What would you Madam ?

   Orb. Why my friends, my Lord !
I would conſult and know, what's to be done.

   Zir. Madam 'tis not ſo ſafe to raiſe the Court ;
things thus unſetled, if you pleaſe to have ――――

   Orb. Where's *Ariaſpes* ?

   Zir. In's dead ſleepe by this time I'm ſure.

   Orb. I know hee is not ! find him inſtantly.

   Zir. I'm gone. ――――   *Turnes back againe.*
But Madam, why make you choyce of him, from whom
if the ſucceſſion meet diſturbance,
all muſt come of danger ?

   Orb. My Lord, I am not yet ſo wiſe, as to be jealous ;
pray diſpute no further.

   Zir. Pardon mee Madam, if before I goe
I muſt vnlock a ſecret unto you ; ſuch a one
as while the King did breathe durſt know no aire,
Zorannes lives.

   Orb. Ha *!*

   Zir. And in the hope of ſuch a day as this
has lingred out a life, ſnatching, to feed
his almoſt famiſh'd eyes,
ſights now and then of you, in a diſguiſe.

   Orb. Strange *!* this night is big with miracle *!*

   Zir. If you did love him, as they ſay you did,

and doe so still; 'tis now within your power.

ORB. I would it were my Lord, but I am now
no private woman, if I did love him once
(and 'tis so long agoe, I have forgot)
my youth and ignorance may well excuse't.

ZIR. Excuse it?

ORB. Yes, excuse it Sir.

ZIR. Though I confesse I lov'd his father much,
and pitie him, yet having offer'd it
unto your thoughts : I have discharg'd a trust;
and zeale shall stray no further.

Your pardon Madam :   *Exit.*   *Queene studies.*

ORB. May be 'tis a plot to keep off *Ariaspes*
greatnesse, which hee must feare, because hee knowes
hee hates him : for these great Statef-men,
that when time has made bold with the King and Subject,
throwing downe all fence that stood betwixt their power
and others right, are on a change,
like wanton Salmons comming in with flouds,
that leap o're wyres and nets, and make their way
to be at the returne to everie one a prey.

>   *Enter* Ziriff, *and* Pasithas *throwing downe the dead*
>   *body of* Ariaspes.

ORB. Ha ! murthered too !
treason —— treason ——

ZIR. But such another word, and halfe so loud,
and th'art. ——

ORB. Why ? thou wilt not murther mee too ?
wilt thou villaine ?

ZIR. I doe not know my temper —— *Discovers himselfe.*
Looke here vaine thing, and see thy sins full blowne :
There's scarce a part in all this face, thou hast
not beene forsworne by, and Heav'n forgive thee for't !
for thee I lost a Father, Countrey, friends,
my selfe almost, for I lay buried long ;
and when there was no use thy love could pay
too great, thou mad'st the principle away :
had I but staid, and not began revenge
till thou had'st made an end of changing,
I had had the Kingdome to have kill'd :
As wantons entring a Garden, take
the first faire flower, they meet, and
treasure't in their laps.
Then seeing more, doe make fresh choyce agen,
throwing in one and one, till at the length
the first poore flower o're-charg'd, with too much weight
withers, and dies :
so hast thou dealt with mee,
and having kill'd mee first, I will kill ——

ORB. Hold —— hold ——
Not for my sake, but *Orbella's* (Sir) a bare
and single death is such a wrong to Justice,
I must needs except against it.
Finde out a way to make mee long a dying,
for death's no punishment, it is the sense,
the paines and feares afore that makes a death :

To thinke what I had had, had I had you,
what I have loft in lofing of my felfe ;
are deaths farre worfe than any you can give :
yet kill mee quickly, for if I have time,
I fhall fo wafh this foule of mine with teares,
make it fo fine, that you would be afrefh
in love with it, and fo perchance I fhould
againe come to deceive you. *Shee rifes up weeping, and hanging downe her head.*

ZIR. So rifes day, blufhing at nights deformitie :
and fo the prettie flowers blubber'd with dew,
and ever wafht with raine, hang downe their heads,
I muft not looke upon her : *(Goes towards him.)*

ORB. Were but the Lillies in this face as frefh
as are the rofes ; had I but innocence
joyn'd to their blufhes, I fhould then be bold,
for when they went on begging they were ne're deni'de,
'Tis but a parting kiffe Sir ————

ZIR. I dare not grant it. ————

ORB. Your hand Sir then, for that's a part I fhall
love after death (if after death wee love)
'caufe it did right the wrong'd *Zorannes*, here ————
        Steps to him, and open the box of poyfon, Zorannes *falls.*
Sleepe, fleepe for ever, and forgotten too,
all but thy ills, which may fucceeding time
remember, as the Sea-man does his marks,
to know what to avoyd, may at thy name
all good men ftart, and bad too, may it prove
infection to the Aire, that people dying of it,
may helpe to curfe thee for mee. *Turnes to the body of* Ariafpes.
Could I but call thee back as eas'ly now ;
but that's a Subject for our teares, not hopes !
there is no piecing Tulips to their ftalks,
when they are once divorc'd by a rude hand ;
all wee can doe is to preferve in water
a little life, and give by courteous Art
what fcanted Nature wants Commiffion for,
that thou fhalt have : for to thy memorie
fuch Tribute of moyft forrow I will pay,
and that fo purifi'd by love, that on thy grave
nothing fhall grow but Violets and Primrofes,
of which too, fome fhall be
of the myfterious number, fo that Lovers fhall
come thither not as to a Tombe, but to an Oracle. *Shee knocks, and raifes the Court.*
        Enter Ladies and Courtiers, as out of their beds.

ORB. Come ! come ! help mee to weep my felfe away,
and melt into a grave, for life is but
repentance nurfe, and will confpire with memorie,
to make my houres my tortures.

ORI. What Scene of forrow's this ? both dead !

ORB. Dead ? I ! and 'tis but halfe death's triumphs this,
the King and Prince lye fomewhere, juft
fuch emptie truncks as thefe.

ORI. The Prince ?
then in griefes burthen I muft beare a part.

SEM. The noble *Ariafpes* —— valiant *Ziriff* too.——*Weeps.*

ORB. Weep'ft thou for him, fond Prodigall ? do'ft know

on whom thou fpend'ft thy teares ? this is the man
to whom wee owe our ills ; the falfe *Zorannes*
difguis'd, not loft ; but kept alive, by fome   *Enter* Pafithas, *furveyes the bodies,*
incenfed Power, to punifh *Perfia* thus :   *findes his Mafter.*
Hee would have kill'd mee too, but Heav'n was juft,
and furnifht mee with meanes, to make him pay
this fcore of villanie, ere hee could doe more.

    PAS. Were you his murth'rer then ? ——   Pafithas *runs at her, kills her, and flies.*
    ORI. Ah mee ! the Queene. ——   *Rub her till fhee come to her felfe.*
    SEM. How doe you Madam ?
    ORB. Well, —— but I was better, and fhall ——   *Dies.*
    SEM. Oh ! fhee is gone for ever.
             Enter Lords in their night gownes, Orfames, Philan.
    ORS. What have wee here ?
a Church-yard ? nothing but filence, and grave ?
    ORI. Oh ! here has been (my Lords)
the blackeft night the *Perfian* world e're knew,
the King and Prince are not themfelves exempt
from this arreft ; but pale and cold, as thefe,
have meafured out their lengths.
    LO. Impoffible ! which way ?
    SEM. Of that wee are as ignorant as you :
for while the Queene was telling of the Storie,
an unknowne villaine here has hurt her fo,
that like a fickly Taper, fhee but made
one flafh, and fo expir'd :
             Enter tearing in Pafithas.
    PHI. Here hee is, but no confeffion.
    OR. Torture muft force him then :
though 'twill indeed, but weakly fatisfie
to know now they are dead, how they did die.
    PHI. Come take the bodies up, and let us all
goe drowne our felves in teares, this maffacre
has left fo torne a ftate, that 'twill be policie
as well as debt, to weep till wee are blinde,
    For who would fee the miferies behinde ?

          L   Epilogue.

Epilogue.

OVr Play is done, and yours doth now begin:
What different Fancies, people now are in?
How strange, and odd a mingle it would make,
If e're they rise; 'twere possible to take
All votes. ———
But as when an authentique Watch is showne,
Each man windes up, and rectifies his owne,
So in our verie Iudgements; first there sits
A grave Grand Iurie on it of Towne-wits;
And they give up their verdict; then agin
The other Iurie of the Court comes in
(And that's of life and death) for each man sees
That oft condemnes, what th'other Iurie frees:
Some three dayes hence, the Ladies of the Towne
Will come to have a Iudgement of their owne:
And after them, their servants; then the Citie,
For that is modest, and is still last wittie.
'Twill be a weeke at least yet e're they have
Resolv'd to let it live, or giv't a grave:
Such difficultie, there is to unite
Opinion; or bring it to be right.

Epilogue for the Court.

Sir :

THat th'abusing of your eare's a crime,
Above th'excuse any six lines in Rhime
Can make, the Poet knowes : I am but sent
T'intreat hee may not be a President,
For hee does thinke that in this place there bee
Many have done't as much and more than hee ;
But here's, hee sayes, the difference of the Fates,
Hee begs a Pardon after't, they Estates.

FINIS.

AGLAURA.

LONDON,
Printed by *Iohn Haviland* for *Thomas Walkley*, and are
to be fold at his fhop at the Signe of the Flying
Horfe betweene York-houfe
and Britaines Burfe. 1638.

Prologue.

Fore Iove, a mightie Seſsions : and I feare,
Though kind laſt Sizes, 'twill be now ſevere ;
For it is thought, and by judicious men,
Aglaura 'ſcap't onely by dying then :
But 'twould be vaine for mee now to indeare,
Or ſpeake unto my Lords, the Iudges here,
They hold their places by condemning ſtill,
And cannot ſhew at once mercie and skill ;
For wit's ſo cruell unto wit, that they
Are thought to want, that find not want i'th' play.
But Ladies you, who never like'd a plot,
But where the Servant had his Miſtreſſe got,
And whom to ſee a Lover dye it grieves,
Although 'tis in worſe language that he lives,
will like't w' are confident, ſince here will bee,
That your Sex ever like'd, varietie.

Prologue to the Court.

TIs ſtrange perchance (you'll thinke) that ſhee that di'de
At Chriſtmas, ſhould at Eaſter be a Bride :
But 'tis a privilege the Poets have,
To take the long-ſince dead out of the grave:
Nor is this all, old Heroës aſleepe,
'Twixt marble coverlets, and ſix foot deepe
In earth, they boldly wake, and make them doe
All they did living here ―――― ſometimes more too,
They give freſh life, reverſe and alter Fate,
And yet more bold, Almightie-like create:
And out of nothing onely to deſie
Reaſon, and Reaſons friend, Philoſophie,
Fame, honour, valour, all that's great, or good,
Or is at leaſt 'mong ſt us, ſo underſtood,
They give, heav'ns theirs, no handſome woman dies,
But if they pleaſe, is ſtrait ſome ſtar i'th' skies―――――
But oh ――――― ―――――
How thoſe poore men of Meetre doe
Flatter themſelves with that, that is not true,
And 'cauſe they can trim up a little proſe,
And ſpoile it handſomly, vainly ſuppoſe
Th'are Omnipotent, can doe all thoſe things
That can be done onely by Gods and Kings.
Of this wild guilt, hee faine would bee thought free,
That writ this Play, and therefore (Sir) by mee,
Hee humbly begs, you would be pleas'd to know,
Aglaura's but repriev'd this night, and though
Shee now appeares upon a Poets call,
Shee's not to live, unleſſe you ſay ſhee ſhall.

ACTUS

ACTUS V. SCENA I.

Enter Ziriff, Paſithas, and Guard: hee places'em : and Exit.
A State ſet out. Enter Ziriff, Jolas, Ariaſpes.

JOL. A Glorious night !
       ARI. Pray Heav'n it prove ſo.
Are wee not there yet ?
  ZIR. 'Tis about this hollow.   *They enter the Cave.*
    ARI. How now ! what region are wee got into ?
the inheritance of night ;
have wee not miſtaken a turning *Ziriff,*
and ſtept into the confines of ſome melancholy
Devílls Territorie ?
    JOL. Sure 'tis a part of the firſt *Chaos,*
that would not ſuffer any change,
    ZIR. No matter Sir, 'tis as proper for our
purpoſe, as the Lobbie for the waiting womans :
ſtay you here, I'le move a little backward,
and ſo wee ſhall be ſure to put him paſt
retreat, you know the word if it be the Prince.   *Ziriff goes to the Doore.*
              Enter King.
    ZIR. Here Sir, follow mee, all's quiet yet.
    KING. Is hee not come then ?
    ZIR. No.
    KING. Where's *Ariaſpes ?*
    ZIR. Waiting within.
    JOL. I doe not like this waiting,
nor this fellowes leaving of us.
    ARI. This place does put odd thoughts into thee;
then thou art in thine owne nature too
as jealous, as Love, or Honour ; weare thy ſword
in readineſſe, and thinke how neere wee are a Crowne.
    ZIR. Revenge ! ——   *Guard ſeiſeth on'em.*
    KING. Ha ! what's this ?
    ZIR. Bring them forth. ——   *Brings them forth.*
    ARI. The King.
    ZIR. Yes, and the Princes friend —— *Diſcovers himſelfe.*
D'you know this face ?
    KING. *Zorannes.*
    ZOR. The verie ſame,
the wrong'd *Zorannes,* —— King ——
D'you ſtare, ——
away with them where I appointed.
    KING. Traytours, let mee goe ;
villaine, thou dar'ſt not doe this ——
    ZOR. Poore Counterfeit;
how faine thou now would'ſt act a King, and art not :
ſtay you, ——   *to Ariaſpes.*
Unhand him, ——   *Whiſpers.*
Leave us now. —— *Exeunt.* *Manet Ariaſp. Zoran.*
    ARI. What does this meane ?
ſure hee does intend the Crowne to mee.
    ZOR. Wee are alone,
follow mee out of the wood, and thou ſhalt be

Master of this againe,
and then best arme and title take it.

ARI. Thy offer is so noble, in gratitude I cannot
but propound gentler conditions,
wee will divide the Empire.

ZOR. Now by my fathers soule,
I doe almost repent my first intents,
and now could kill thee scurvily, for thinking
if I had a minde to rule,
I would not rule alone,
let not thy easie faith (lost man)
foole thee into so dull an heresie;
Orbella is our quarrell, and I have thought it fit,
that love should have a nobler way of Justice,
than Revenge, or Treason.
If thou dar'st dye handsomly, follow mee.   *Exeunt.*   *And enter both agen.*

ZOR. There,———   *Gives him his sword.*

ARI. Extremely good ; Nature tooke paines I sweare,
the villaine and the brave are mingled handsomely :———

ZIR. 'Twas Fate that tooke it, when it decreed
wee two should meet, nor shall they mingle now,
wee are but brought together strait to part. ——— *Fight.*

ARI. Some Devill sure has borrowed this shape,
my sword ne're staid thus long to finde an entrance.

ZIR. To guiltie men, all that appeare is Devill ;
come trifler, come, ——— *Fight.*

ARI. Dog, thou hast it.

ZIR. Why then it seemes my star's as great as his,
I smile at thee,   *Ariaspes pants, and*
thou now would'st have me kill thee,   *runs at him to catch*
and 'tis a courtesie I cannot afford thee,   *his sword.*
I have bethought my selfe, there will be use
of thee,——— *Pasithas* ——— to the rest with him.   *Exit.*
     Enter Pasithas, *and two of the Guard.* ——— *Exeunt.*
         Enter Thersames.

THER. The Dog-star's got up high, it should be late:
and sure by this time every waking eare,
and watchfull eye is charm'd ; and yet mee thought
a noyse of weapons struck my eare just now.
'Twas but my Fancie sure, and were it more,
I would not tread one step, that did not lead
to my *Aglaura*, stood all his Guard betwixt,
with lightning in their hands.
Danger, thou Dwarfe drest up in Giants clothes,
that shew'st far off still greater than thou art,
goe, terrifie the simple, and the guiltie, such
as with false Opticks still doe looke upon thee :
but fright not Lovers, wee dare looke on thee
in thy worst shapes, and meet thee in them too. ———
Stay, these trees I made my marke, 'tis hereabouts,
——— Love guide mee but right this night,
and Lovers shall restore thee back againe
those eyes the Poets tooke so boldly from thee.   *Exit.*
        A Taper, Table out.
   Enter Aglaura, *with a Torch in one hand, a Dagger in the other.*

AGL. How ill this does become this hand ? much worse

                                  this

this fuits with this, one of the two fhould goe :
The fhee within mee fayes, it muft be this,———
honour fayes this —— and honour is *Therfames* friend.
What is that fhee then, is it not a thing ·
that fets a price, not upon mee, but on
life in my name, leading mee into doubt,
which when 'thas done, it cannot light mee out ?
For feare does drive to Fate, or Fate if wee
doe flie, ore-takes, and holds us, till or death,
or infamie, or both doe feife us.   *Puts out the light.*
Ha ! ——would 'twere in agen. Antiques & ftrange mifhapes,
fuch as the Porter to my Soule, mine Eye,
was ne're acquainted with, fancie lets in,
like a difrouted multitude, by fome ftrange accident
piec'd together; feare now afrefh comes on,
and charges Love too home.
—— Hee comes, hee comes.——*A little noyfe below.*
woman, if thou would'ft be the Subject
of mans wonder, not his fcorne hereafter,——.
———— now fhew thy felfe.
          Enter Therfames *from the vault, fhe ftabs him as he rifeth.*
    THER. Unkindly done ——
    AGL. The Princes voyce, defend it Goodneffe ?
    THER. What art thou that thus poorely
haft deftroy'd a life ?
    AGL. Oh fad miftake, 'tis hee ?
    THER. Haft thou no voyce ?
    AGL. I would I had not, nor a being neither.
    THER. *Aglaura*, it cannot be ?
    AGL. Oh ftill beleeve fo, Sir,
for 'twas not I indeed, but fatall Love.
    THER. Loves wounds us'd to be gentler than thefe were,
the paines they give us have fome pleafure
in them, and that thefe have not.   *Enter* Ziriff *with a taper.*
Oh doe not fay 'twas you, for that does wound agen :
guard mee my better Angell,
doe I wake ? my eyes (fince I was man)
ne're met with any object gave them fo much trouble,
I dare not aske neither to be fatisfied,
fhee lookes fo guiltily ——
    AGL. Why doe you ftare and wonder at a thing
that you your felfe have made thus miferable ?
    ZIR. Good gods, and I o'the partie too.
    AGL. Did you not tell mee that the King this night
meant to attempt my honour, that our condition
would not admit of middle wayes, and that wee muft
fend them to graves, or lye our felves in duft ?
    ZIR. Unfortunate miftake!   *Ziriff knocks.*
I never did intend our fafetie by thy hands :   *Enter* Pafithas.
Pafithas, goe inftantly and fetch *Andrages*
from his bed ; how is it with you Sir ?
    THER. As with the befieg'd :
my foule is fo befet it does not know,
whether 't had beft to make a defperate
fally out by this port or not ?
    AGL. Sure I fhall turne ftatue here.

THER. If thou do'st love mee, weepe not *Aglaura*:
all thofe are drops of bloud, and flow from mee.

ZIR. Now all the gods defend this way of expiation,
Think'ft thou thy crime, *Aglaura* would be leffe,
by adding to it? or canft thou hope
to fatisfie thofe powers, whom great fins
doe difpleafe, by doing greater.

AGL. Difcourteous courtefie!
I had no other meanes left mee than this,
to let *Therfames* know I would doe nothing
to him, I would not doe unto my felfe,
and that thou takeft away.

THER. Friend, bring mee a little nearer,
I finde a kinde of willingneffe to ftay,
and finde that willingneffe fomething obey'd.
My bloud now it perfwades it felfe
you did not call in earneft,
makes not fuch hafte ———

AGL. Oh my deareft Lord,
this kindneffe is fo full of crueltie,
puts fuch an uglineffe on what I have done,
that when I looke upon it, needs muft fright
mee from my felfe, and which is more infufferable,
I feare from you.

THER. Why fhould that fright thee, which moft comforts mee?
I glorie in it, and fhall fmile i'th' grave,
to thinke our love was fuch, that nothing
but it felfe could e're deftroy it.

AGL. Deftroy it? can it have ever end?
will you not be thus courteous then in the other world?
fhall wee not be together there as here?

THER. I cannot tell whether I may or not.

AGL. Not tell?

THER. No:
The Gods thought mee unworthy of thee here,
and when thou art more pure,
why fhould I not more doubt it?

AGL. Becaufe if I fhall be more pure,
I fhall be then more fit for you.
Our Priefts affure us an *Elyfium*,
and can that be *Elyfium* where true Lovers
muft not meet? Thofe Powers that made our loves,
did they intend them mortall,
would fure have made them of a courfer ftuffe,
would they not my Lord? ———

THER. Prethee fpeake ftill,
this mufique gives my foule fuch pleafing bufineffe,
takes it fo wholly up, it findes not leafure to
attend unto the fummons death does make;
yet they are loud and peremptorie now,
and I can onely ———   *Faints.*

AGL. Some pitying Power infpire mee with
a way to follow him: heart wilt thou not
breake it of thy felfe.

ZIR. My griefes befot mee:
his foule will faile out with this purple tide,

and I shall here be found staring
after't, like a man that's come too short o'th' ship,
and's left behinde upon the land. *Shee swounes.*

Enter Andrages.

Oh welcome, welcome, here lyes, *Andrages*,
alas too great a triall for thy art.

AND. There's life in him: from whence these wounds?

ZIR. Oh 'tis no time for storie.

AND. 'Tis not mortall my Lord, bow him gently,
and help mee to infuse this into him;
the soule is but asleepe, and not gone forth.

THER. Oh —— oh: ——————

ZIR. Hearke, the Prince does live.

THER. What e're thou art hast given mee now a life,
and with it all my cares and miseries,
expect not a reward, no not a thanks.
If thou would'st merit from mee,
(yet wh'would be guiltie of so lost an action)
restore mee to my quietnesse agen,
for life and that are most incompatible.

ZIR. Still in despaires:
I did not thinke till now 'twas in the power
of Fortune to have robb'd *Thersames* of himselfe,
for pitie, Sir, and reason live;
if you will die, die not *Aglaura's* murther'd;
that's not so handsome: at least die not
her murthered, and her murtherer too;
for that will surely follow. Looke up, Sir,
this violence of Fortune cannot last ever:
who knowes but all these clouds are shadowes,
to set off your fairer dayes, if it growes blacker,
and the stormes doe rise, this harbour's alwayes open.

THER. What say'st thou, *Aglaura?*

AGL. What sayes *Andrages?*

AND. Madam, would Heaven his mind would admit
as easie cure, as his body will;
'Twas onely want of bloud,
and two houres rest restores him to himselfe.

ZIR. And by that time it may be Heaven
will give our miseries some ease:
come Sir, repose upon a bed,
there's time enough to day.

THER. Well, I will still obey,
though I must feare it will be with mee,
but as 'tis with tortured men,
whom States preserve onely to wrack agen. *Exeunt.*

Take off table.

Enter Ziriff *with a taper.*

ZIR. All fast too, here
They sleepe to night
i'their winding sheets I thinke, there's such
a generall quiet.
Oh! here's light I warrant you:
for lust does take as little rest, as care, or age.
Courting her glasse, I sweare, fie! that's a flatterer Madam,
in mee you shall see trulier what you are. *He knocks. Enter Queene.*

ORB.

ORB. What make you up at this strange houre my Lord?

ZIR. My businesse is my boldnesse warrant,
(Madam)
and I could well afford t'have beene without it now,
had Heav'n so pleas'd.

ORB. 'Tis a sad Prologue,
what followes in the name of vertue?

ZIR. The King————

ORB. I: what of him? is well is hee not?

ZIR. Yes,————
If to be on's journey to the other world
be to be well, hee is.

ORB. Why hee's not dead, is hee?

ZIR. Yes, Madam, dead.

ORB. How? where?

ZIR. I doe not know particulars.

ORB. Dead!

ZIR. Yes(Madam).

ORB. Art sure hee's dead?

ZIR. Madam I know him as certainly dead,
as I know you too must die hereafter

ORB. Dead!

ZIR. Yes, dead.

ORB. Wee must all die,
the Sisters spin no cables for us mortalls;
th'are threds; and Time, and chance————
trust mee I could weep now,
but watrie distillations doe but ill on graves,
they make the lodging colder.   *Shee knocks.*

ZIR. What would you Madam?

ORB. Why my friends, my Lord;
I would consult and know, what's to be done.

ZIR.(Madam) 'tis not so safe to raise the Court,
things thus unsetled, if you please to have————

ORB. Where's *Ariaspes*?

ZIR. In's dead sleepe by this time sure.

ORB. I know hee is not! find him instantly.

ZIR. I'm gone.————   *Turnes back againe.*
But(Madam) why make you choyce of him, from whom
if the succession meet disturbance,
all must come of danger?

ORB. My Lord, I am not yet so wise, as to be
jealous; pray dispute no further.

ZIR. Pardon mee(Madam)if before I goe
I must vnlock a secret to you; such a one
as while the King did breathe durst know no aire,
Zorannes lives.

ORB. Ha!

ZIR. And in the hope of such a day as this
has lingred out a life, snatching, to feed
his almost famish'd eyes,
sights now and then of you, in a disguise.

ORB. Strange! this night is big with miracle!

ZIR. If you did love him, as they say you did,
and doe so still; 'tis now within your power:

ORB. I would it were, my Lord, but I am now

no private woman, if I did love him once,
(as 'tis so long agoe, I have forgot)
my youth and ignorance may well excuse't.

   Z I R. Excuse it?

   O R B. Yes, excuse it Sir.

   Z I R. Though I confesse I lov'd his father much,
and pitie him, yet having offer'd it
unto your thoughts : I have discharg'd a trust ;
and zeale shall stray no further.
(Your pardon Madam:)   *Exit.*

   O R B. May be 'tis but a plot to keep off *Ariaspes*
greatnesse, which hee must feare, because hee knowes
hee hates him : for these great States-men,
that when time has made bold with the King
and Subject, throwing downe all fence
that stood betwixt their power
and others right, are on a change,
like wanton Salmons comming in with flouds,
that leap o're wyres and nets, and make their way
to be at the returne to everie one a prey.

      Enter Ziriff.

   Z I R. Looke here vaine thing, and see thy sins full blowne :
There's scarce a part in all this face, thou hast
not beene forsworne by, and Heav'n forgive thee for't *!*
for thee I lost a Father, Countrey, friends,
my selfe almost, for I lay buried long ;
and when there was no use thy love could pay
too great, thou mad'st the principle away : —— *Prompt.* ——
   As wantons entring a Garden, take
the first faire flower they meet, and
treasure't in their laps.
Then seeing more, doe make fresh choyce agen,
throwing in one and one, till at the length
the first poore flower o're-charg'd, with too much weight
withers, and dies :
so hast thou dealt with mee,
and having kill'd mee first, I will kill ——

   O R B. Hold —— hold ——
Not for my sake, but *Orbella's* (Sir) a bare
and single death is such a wrong to Justice,
I must needs except against it.
Finde out a way to make mee long a dying ;
for death's no punishment, it is the sense,
the paines and feares afore that makes a death :
To thinke what I had had, had I had you,
what I have lost in losing of my selfe ;
are deaths farre worse than any you can give :
yet kill mee quickly, for if I have time,
I shall so wash this soule of mine with teares,
make it so fine, that you would be afresh
in love with it, and so perchance I should
againe come to deceive you.   *Shee rises up weeping, and hanging downe her head.*

   Z I R. So rises day, blushing at nights deformitie :
and so the prettie flowers blubber'd with dew,
and over-washt with raine, hang downe their heads,

           I must

I muſt not looke upon her.   (*Queene goes towards him.*)

ORB. Were but the Lillies in this face as freſh
as are the roſes ; had I but innocence
joyn'd to theſe bluſhes, I ſhould then be bold,
for when they went a begging they were ne're deni'de,
'Tis but a parting kiſſe Sir ———

Enter Paſithas, *and two Guard.*

ZIR. I dare not grant it. —— *Paſithas* —away with her.

A bed put out : Therſames *and* Aglaura *on it,* Andrages *by.*

THER. Shee wake't mee with a ſigh,
and yet ſhee ſleepes her ſelfe, ſweet Innocence,
can it be ſinne to love this ſhape,
and if it be not, why am I perſecuted thus ? ———
ſhee ſighs agen, ſleepe that drownes all cares,
cannot I ſee charme loves ? bleſt pillowes,
through whoſe fineneſſe does appeare
the violets, lillies, and the roſes
you are ſtuft withall, to whoſe ſoftneſſe
I owe the ſweet of this repoſe,
permit mee to leave with you this, —— *Kiſſes them, ſhee wakes.*
ſee if I have not wake't her,
ſure I was borne, *Aglaura,* to deſtroy
thy quiet.

AGL. Mine, my Lord,
call you this drowſineſſe a quiet then ?
belee.e mee, Sir, 'twas an intruder I much
ſtruggled with, and have to thanke a dreame,
not you, that it thus left mee.

THER. A dreame ! what dreame, my Love ?

AGL. I dream't (Sir) it was day,
and the feare you ſhould be found here.

Enter Ziriff.

ZIR. Awake ; how is it with you, Sir ?

THER. Well, extremely well, ſo well, that had I now
no better a remembrancer than paine,
I ſhould forget I e're was hurt,
thanks to Heaven, and good *Andrages.*

ZIR. And more than thanks I hope wee yet ſhall
live to pay him. How old's the night?

AND. Far-ſpent I feare, my Lord.

ZIR. I have a cauſe that ſhould be heard
yet ere day breake, and I muſt needs entreat
you Sir to be the Judge in't.

THER. What cauſe, *Zorannes ?*

ZIR. When you have promis'd ———

THER. 'Twere hard I ſhould denie thee any thing.   —— *Exit* Zorannes.
Know'ſt thou, *Andrages,* what hee meanes ?

AND. Nor cannot gheſſe, Sir,   —— *Draw in the bed.*
I read a trouble in his face, when firſt
hee left you, but underſtood it not.

Enter Zorannes, *King,* Ariaſpes, Jolas, *Queene, and two or three Guard.*

ZOR. Have I not pitcht my nets like a good Huntſman ?
Looke, Sir, the nobleſt of the Herd are here.

THER. I am aſtoniſhed.

ZOR. This place is yours. ——— *Helps him up.*

THER. What would'ſt thou have mee doe.

ZOR?

ZOR. Remember, Sir, your promise,
I could doe all I have to doe, alone;
but Justice is not Justice unlesse't be justly done:
here then I will begin, for here began my wrongs.
This woman (Sir) was wondrous faire, and wondrous
kinde, —— I, faire and kinde, for so the storie runs,
she gave me looke for looke, and glance for glance,
and every sigh like eccho's was return'd,
wee sent up vow by vow, promise on promise,
so thick and strangely multiplyed,
that sure we gave the heavenly Registers
their businesse, and other mortalls oaths
then went for nothing, wee felt each others paines,
each others joyes, thought the same thought,
and spoke the verie same;
wee were the same, and I have much adoe
to thinke shee could be ill, and I not
be so too, and after this, all this (Sir)
shee was false, lov'd him, and him,
and had I not begun revenge,
till shee had made an end of changing,
I had had the Kingdome to have kill'd,
what does this deserve?

THER. A punishment hee best can make
that suffered the wrong.

ZOR. I thanke you, Sir,
for him I will not trouble you,
his life is mine, I won it fairly,
and his is yours, hee lost it fouly to you ══════
to him, Sir, now:
A man so wicked that he knew no good,
but so as't made his sins the greater for't.
Those ills, which singly acted bred despaire
in others, he acted daily, and ne're thought
upon them.
The grievance each particular has against him
I will not meddle with, it were to give him
a long life, to give them hearing,
Ile onely speake my owne.
First then the hopes of all my youth,
and a reward which Heaven had settled on mee,
(if holy contracts can doe any thing)
hee ravisht from mee, kill'd my father,
Aglaura's father, Sir, would have whor'd my sister,
and murther'd my friend, this is all:
and now your sentence, Sir.

THER. We have no punishment can reach these crimes:
therefore 'tis justest sure to send him where
th'are wittier to punish than we are here:
and cause repentance oft stops that proceeding,
a sudden death is sure the greatest punishment.

ZOR. I humbly thanke you, Sir.

KING. What a strange glasse th'have shew'd me now my selfe
in; our sins like to our shadowes,
when our day is in its glorie scarce appear'd,
towards our evening how great and monstrous
they are.

ZOR. Is this all you have to say?——— *Drawes.*

THER. Hold:——— now goe you up.

ZOR. What meane you, Sir?

THER. Nay, I denyed not you,———
That all thy accusations are just,
I must acknowledge,
and to these crimes, I have but this t'oppose,
hee is my Father, and thy Soveraigne. ———
'Tis wickednesse (deare Friend) wee goe about
to punish, and when w'have murther'd him,
what difference is there 'twixt him and
our selves, but that hee first was wicked? ———
Thou now would'st kill him 'cause he kill'd thy Father,
and when th'hast kill'd, have not I the selfe same
quarrell?

ZOR. Why Sir, you know you would your selfe
have done it.

THER. True: and therefore 'tis I beg his life,
there was no way for mee to have
redeem'd th'intent, but by a reall
saving of it.
If hee did ravish from thee thy *Orbella,*
remember that that wicked issue had
a noble parent, Love, ——— Remember
how he lov'd *Zorannes* when he was *Ziriff,*———
ther's something due to that. ———
If you must needs have bloud for your revenge,
take it here ——— despise it not *Zorannes:*
The gods themselves, whose greatnesse
makes the greatnesse of our sins,
and heightens 'em above what wee can doe
unto each other, accept of sacrifice
for what wee doe 'gainst them,
why should not you, and 'tis much thriftier too:
you cannot let out life there, but my honour
goes, and all the life you can take here,
posteritie will give mee back agen;
see, *Aglaura* weepes:
that would have beene ill Rhetorique in mee,
but where it is, it cannot but perswade.

ZOR. Th'have thaw'd the ice about my heart;
I know not what to doe.

KING. Come downe, come downe, I will be King agen,
there's none so fit to be the Judge of this
as I; the life you shew'd such zeale to save,
I here could willingly returne you back;
but that's the common price of all revenge.

    Enter Guard, Orsames, Philan, *Courtiers,* Orithie, Semanthe.

JOL. ARI. Ha, ha, ha: how they looke now?

ZOR. Death: what's this?

THER. Betray'd agen;
all th'ease our Fortune gives our miseries is hope,
and that still proving false growes part of it.

KING. From whence this Guard?

ARI. Why Sir, I did corrupt, while we were his prisoners,
one of his owne to raise the Court; shallow soules,

Be ready Courtiers, and Guard, with their swords drawne, at the brests of the Prisoners.

Zorannes turnes away.

that thought wee could not countermine ;
come Sir, y'are in good posture to dispatch them.

KING. Lay hold upon his instrument :
Fond man, do'st thinke I am in love with villany ?
all the service they can doe mee here
is but to let these see the right I doe
them now is unconstrain'd, then thus I doe proceed.
Upon the place *Zorannes* lost his life,
I vow to build a tomb, and on that tomb
I vow to pay three whole yeares penitence,
if in that time I finde that heaven and you
can pardon ; I shall finde agen the way
to live amongst you.

THER. Sir, be not so cruell to your selfe, this is an age.

KING. 'Tis now irrevocable, thy Fathers lands
I give thee back agen, and his commands,
and with them leave to weare the Tyara,
that man there has abus'd. ———
To you *Orbella*,
who it seemes are foule as well as I,
I doe prescribe the selfe same physick
I doe take my selfe :
but in another place, and for a longer time,
Diana's Nunnerie.

ORB. Above my hopes.

KING. For you, who still have beene
the ready instrument of all my cruelties,
and there have cancell'd all the bonds of brother,
perpetuall banishment : nor, should
this line expire, shall thy right have a place.

ARI. Hell and Furies. ———   *Exit.*

KING. Thy crimes deserve no lesse, yet 'cause thou wert
Heavens instrument to save my life,
thou onely hast that time of banishment,
I have of penitence. ———   *Comes downe.*   Ziriff *offers to kisse the Kings hand.*

JOL. May it be plague and famine here till I returne.
No: thou shalt not yet forgive mee :

KING. *Aglaura*, thus I freely part with thee,
and part with all fond flames and warme desires ;
I cannot feare new agues in my bloud
since I have overcome the charmes
thy beautie had, no other ever can
have so much power, *Thersames*, thou look'st pale,
is't want of rest ?

THER. No Sir ; but that's a storie for your eare ———   *They whisper.*

ORS. A strange and happie change.

ORI. All joyes wait on you ever.

AGL. *Orithie*,
how for thy sake now could I wish
Love were no Mathematick point,
but would admit division, that *Thersames* might,
though at my charge, pay thee the debt hee owes thee.

ORI. Madam, I loved the Prince, not my selfe ;
since his vertues have their full rewards,
I have my full desires.

KING. What miracles of preservation have wee had ?

O   how

how wifely have the ftars prepar'd you for felicitie ?
nothing endeares a good more than the contemplation
of the difficultie wee had to attaine to it :
but fee, Nights Empire's out,
and a more glorious aufpitioufly does begin ;
let us goe ferve the gods, and then prepare
for jollitie, this day Ile borrow from my vowes,
nor fhall it have a common celebration,
fince 't muft be,
a high record to all pofteritie. ——— *Exeunt omnes.*

Epilogue.

PLayes are like Feafts, and everie Act fhould bee
Another Courfe, and ftill varietie :
But in good faith provifion of wit
Is growne of late fo difficult to get,
That doe wee what wee can, w'are not able,
Without cold meats to furnifh out the Table.
Who knowes but it was needleffe too ? may bee
'Twas here, as in the Coach-mans trade, and hee
That turnes in the leaft compaffe, fhewes moft Art :
How e're, the Poet hopes (Sir) for his part,
You'll like not thofe fo much, who fhew their skill
In entertainment, as who fhew their will.

FINIS.

The following blank pages in this copy have been inserted to allow for a better binding.